CHAMPION

a memoir of tennis and teamwork

ASH BARTY

Young Readers Edition

ASH BARTY

CHAMPION
a memoir of tennis and teamwork

Young Readers Edition

HarperCollins*Children's Books*

Aboriginal and Torres Strait Islander readers are respectfully advised this book contains names and descriptions of people who have died.

HarperCollins*Children'sBooks*

HarperCollins*Publishers*
Australia • Brazil • Canada • France • Germany • Holland • India
Italy • Japan • Mexico • New Zealand • Poland • Spain • Sweden
Switzerland • United Kingdom • United States of America

HarperCollins acknowledges the Traditional Custodians
of the land upon which we live and work, and pays respect
to Elders past and present.

First published in Australia in 2023
by HarperCollins*Publishers* Australia Pty Limited
Gadigal Country
Level 19, 201 Elizabeth Street, Sydney NSW 2000
ABN 36 009 913 517
harpercollins.com.au

Copyright © Bartig Pty Ltd 2023

The right of Ashleigh Barty to be identified as the author of this work
has been asserted by her in accordance with the *Copyright Amendment
(Moral Rights) Act 2000.*

This work is copyright. Apart from any use as permitted under
the *Copyright Act 1968*, no part may be reproduced, copied, scanned,
stored in a retrieval system, recorded, or transmitted, in any form or
by any means, without the prior written permission of the publisher.

A catalogue record for this book is available
from the National Library of Australia

ISBN 978 1 4607 6273 8 (paperback)
ISBN 978 1 4607 1530 7 (ebook)

Cover design by Louisa Maggio, HarperCollins Design Studio
Cover image © Tennis Australia/Mark Dadswell
Typeset in Adobe Garamond Pro by Kelli Lonergan
Printed and bound in Australia by McPherson's Printing Group

For Mum, Dad, Sara and Ali.
Without their love and sacrifice,
the best journey of my life never begins.

For you,
Be brave
Be courageous
Be authentic
and most importantly,
Enjoy your unique journey.

Contents

Ash's Journey to WTA World #1	viii
Before Anything and Everything	1
My Mr Miyagi	11
Black Skin, Red Rocks	25
Schoolwork and Broken Hearts	38
The Detroit of Belgium	50
Good Habits	60
Wildcards	66
Big, Ugly Tears	75
A B C D	88
Faster, Flatter	96
The Wolves of Wimbledon	105
Attacking the Bend	119

Toothaches and Toilet Breaks	129
Bullrings and Baguettes	142
Mortgages and Monkey Bars	153
Spit the Dummy	162
Zoom Zoom	177
25 Per Cent Effort	187
Today, Love Won	205
Triumph and Disaster	215
The Last Summer	232
Why, Not When	255
Postscript	263
Thank You	273
Photo Credits	275

Ash's Journey to WTA World #1

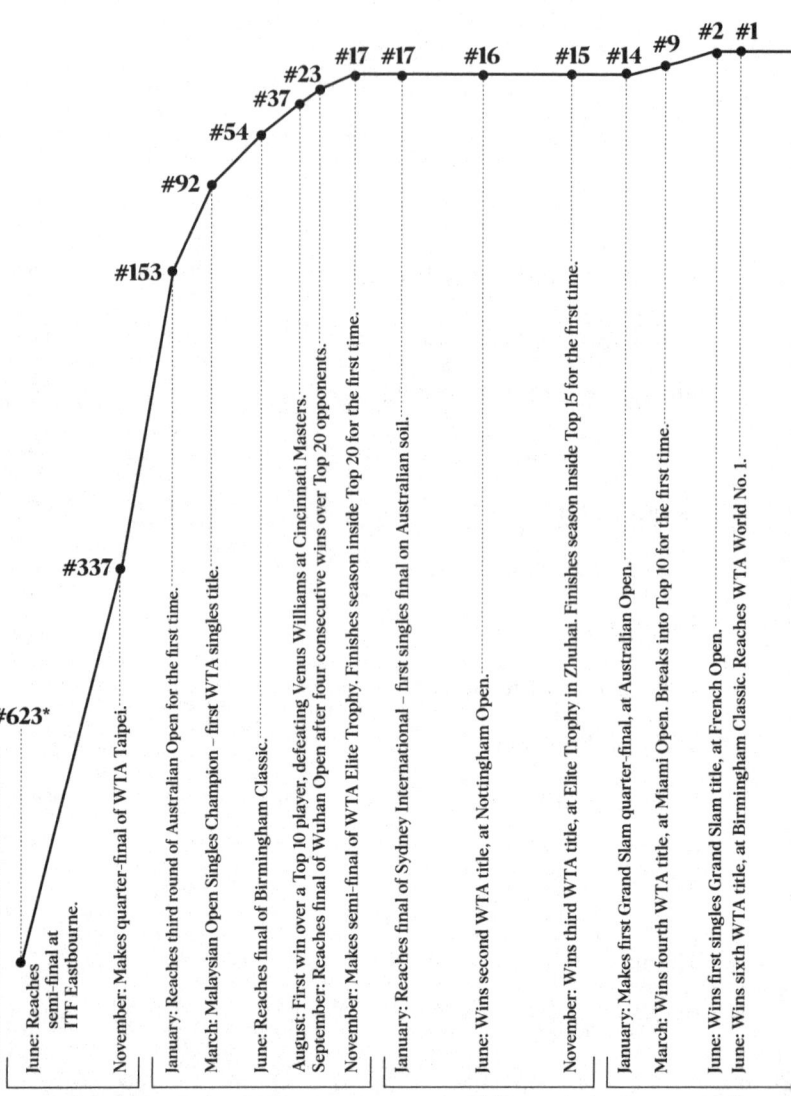

Career Highlights
3 Grand Slam singles titles
1 Grand Slam doubles title
12 WTA singles titles
11 WTA doubles titles
Olympic bronze medal
  for mixed doubles

Ash held the WTA World No. 1 ranking for 114 consecutive weeks, the fourth-longest streak in tour history, behind Steffi Graf (186 weeks), Serena Williams (also 186) and Martina Navratilova (156).

In all, Ash spent 121 weeks at No. 1, the seventh most in WTA tour history, surpassed only by Steffi Graf, Martina Navratilova, Serena Williams, Chris Evert, Martina Hingis and Monica Seles.

#2 #1 #1   #1 #1   #1   #1   #1 #1 #1 #1   #1   #1 #1   #1

2020

- August: Drops to WTA World No. 2.
- September: After US Open, returns to WTA World No. 1.
- November: Wins seventh WTA title, at WTA Finals. Finishes WTA Year-End World No. 1 for the first time.
- January: Wins eighth WTA title, at Adelaide International – first WTA singles title in Australia.
- January: Makes semi-final at Australian Open for the first time.
- From March to November: Does not compete due to Covid-19 pandemic.
- November: Finishes second consecutive year as WTA Year-End World No. 1.

2021

- January: Wins ninth WTA title, at Melbourne Summer Series.
- April: Wins tenth WTA title, at Miami Open.
- April: Wins eleventh WTA title, at Porsche Tennis Grand Prix in Stuttgart.
- July: Wimbledon Ladies' Singles Champion – second Grand Slam singles title.
- August: Wins thirteenth WTA title, at Cincinnati Masters.
- November: Finishes third consecutive year as WTA Year-End World No. 1.

2022

- January: Wins fourteenth WTA title, at Adelaide International.
- January: Wins Australian Open – third Grand Slam singles title.
- March: Announces retirement from professional tennis.

*WTA rankings as per the ranking cycle following that tournament.

Before Anything and Everything

I was born at Ipswich Hospital on 24 April 1996. I arrived four days late with hip sockets that didn't form properly. I had to wear these stirrups that kept my little knees up, as if I was squatting at all times.

I'm told I hated those stirrups, pushing and kicking against them, always trying to get free. Once my hips settled down, I was put in a Jolly Jumper, and apparently that was my first love. If I caught sight of that thing, I'd immediately cry for it. I was a bouncy little thing, I guess, eager to fly up and see beyond my horizon.

I was raised in a brick house with orange walls, a brown tile roof and beige carpet. We lived in a place called Springfield, half an hour away from Brisbane. There are no big busy roads cutting through it – it is a lush and quiet place filled with jacarandas and palms and spindly gums.

My parents met while playing a social game of golf. My mum, Josie, has always played for fun, but my dad, Robert, took the sport a little more seriously than most. Dad's a country boy from Bowen, in north Queensland, and he was driven hard by his strict father.

As a young man, Dad was set to play golf for the University of Houston, a springboard to a professional career, until his father stepped in: 'There's no way you're going to America.'

The boy who took Dad's place went on to join the international tour. Meanwhile, Dad's dream was snuffed out before it caught fire. Being the stubborn person he is, Dad barely picked up a golf club for 25 years. He went on to build a career at the State Library of Queensland instead.

Mum is one of six kids of English migrants, and for most of her professional life she was a radiographer working at Ipswich Hospital. She's the emotional member of our family. The one who cries at the drop of a hat. The clumsy one who needs reminders. In our house, when I was growing up, there was a rule: 'If you're five minutes early, you're ten minutes late.' We made fun of Mum, who was the relaxed one – but in truth she never showed up late for anything. She just had no interest in being 15 minutes early like us!

Importantly, she was the person I sat with when I was sad, who would scratch my head and hold me in her arms.

When I wasn't inside watching *The Simpsons* or *The Brady Bunch* or *The Nanny*, or playing Pokémon on my Nintendo Game Boy, I was out in the garden with Mum. We would go for drives on the weekend and we'd almost always end up at a local nursery, where I could pick out a $1 flower and then go home and plant it in the garden. We'd garden, play with the dogs, or we would read together in the shade. It was simple and comforting, and sparked my love for finding happiness in small things. Mum used to go for morning walks – she still does – and always with her earphones in. She strolled the streets, humming and softly singing to herself. I would tell her she looked weird, but she would just smile serenely because she knew what worked best in her world.

Compared to Mum, Dad was always the organised one. The structured one. Clean. Efficient.

I have that in me too. I'm the kind of person who gets home from a trip and unpacks everything before doing anything else. All bags emptied – immediately.

Some people call it fussy, others call it obsessive-compulsive. The latter term gets thrown around loosely, but not with Dad. He told me once that back when he was a teenager, he needed to learn a particular bunker shot. His coach told him to stay in the sand trap practising that one shot until the action was muscle memory. Dad took that too seriously, and kept swinging until his hands bled. He's struggled with that obsessive thinking his whole life, and with depression. We have that in common.

I think Dad saw a lot of himself in me as I grew up. He was a big softie, really, who wanted nothing more than to see me having fun, laughing and smiling and carefree. I guess he was just my best mate.

I suppose my big sisters were my mates too. But I used to annoy Ali and Sara as much as possible. Do you know the game called 'corners'? I would sit in the middle seat in the back of the car, and every time we turned at a roundabout or took a sharp left or right, I would hurl my body in the opposite direction, trying to crush one sister or the other into the car door.

'Ash, stop it,' I'd hear.

'Ash, stop it,' they'd groan.

'Ash, STOP IT!' they'd snap. And that was when I knew I had them.

Here we go, I'd think, practically rubbing my hands together. *Let's see how far we can take this.*

That was particularly true for Ali, the middle child, who is three years older than me. We grew up sleeping in bunk beds: me on the bottom, her on top. Ali is the kindest, most beautiful, sensitive soul – and I used that against her without mercy. What did we fight over? The breakfast bowl we wanted to use. The first piece of chicken at dinner. The choice of TV show at night. *Whatever you have, I'm going to take it*, I would think. *Because I know you won't fight for it.*

If it was time to clean up, I would hide under the bed and, when caught, pretend to be cleaning under there. I threw an animal encyclopaedia at Ali once – helicoptered it right at her head – but I missed and put a hole in the wall. We joined forces briefly to hide the evidence, covering it with a poster. *Job well done. Shake on it, mate.*

Mum immediately identified it as hung in a strange place.

I betrayed my sister instantly. 'Ali did it!'

We went to Woodcrest State College, which was three kilometres away from home. At some point on the walk home most days, I would drop my schoolbag and simply walk away, or run off. I didn't want to carry it, and I knew that Sara, five years older than me, would have to chase after me since I couldn't cross the street myself – meaning Ali would have to carry my bag.

Ali gave up a lot for me. When I started playing tennis, she gave up netball and decided to learn tennis instead, because it would be easier for Mum and Dad. Later, when I needed more coaching, Ali gave up her private lesson so that we could afford it. Ali was the last person in the family to beat me at tennis, when I was eight and she was 11. And she never played me again. She retired against me with that win – and while that makes me annoyed, if anyone is going to hold victory over me forever, I'm glad it's her. She earned it.

I never clashed with Sara, and not just because she's older. She's simply stronger than me, and smarter than me too. Far smarter, in fact. I never wanted to risk getting on her bad side. We've never had a fight in our lives.

When you're a little kid, your big sister is the one doing everything for the first time. The first to have issues with friends at school. The first to have a boyfriend. The first to go to university. The first to solve every problem. Whenever I met a bumpy road I didn't know how to negotiate, I knew Sara would show me the way. She's the tough one. The pragmatic one.

But our family was far more than just the five of us. My cousins were my mates, and there were dozens of them, and we saw them every weekend.

Family before anything and everything – that's what we were taught.

We felt that most every spring school holidays on North Stradbroke Island. A trip to Straddie meant camping in tents or staying in caravans and cabins, and scores of children with nothing to do but chill and swim. I would go fishing with the boys – my uncles – from early morning to late afternoon. They would invite me and often not the other young cousins, because they knew I wouldn't lose interest or bellyache, and that I would bait my own hook and help pump for yabbies on the flats, and reel in the whiting and the bream from the blue water off the white-sand beaches.

I loved my Straddie uniform: long board shorts, no shirt and a backwards cap. When Mum finally forced me into a top, it was one of those ugly long-sleeved fishing ones with bright colours and pictures of big fish.

For ten days every September it was heaven there. We'd be up at dawn, explore all day, then we'd have 'foursies'. Just after three o'clock, we'd sit around and slowly prepare a long snack – maybe a cheese board and crackers – and we would talk and laugh. It signified that 4 pm was approaching and playtime was over. You have your foursies, you have your shower, you eat your dinner, you go to bed. You close your eyes and dream deeply while the water laps at the shore and the Milky Way dances up above and the Earth spins and the sun returns and you do it all again.

My Mr Miyagi

My sisters had played netball, but I didn't want that. I saw a hockey field on the way to their match one day and was interested – I liked the idea of hitting people with a stick – but there was no way Mum would get on board. Not many girls played cricket in those days, but I knew there had to be a bat-and-ball sport for me.

Mum and Dad had always watched tennis and loved it, but they'd never played. They had heard from a family friend about this bloke called Jim Joyce, a tennis coach. He was apparently a good man, running a sound local business. And so, Dad drove me one morning down to the West Brisbane Tennis Centre.

The West Brisbane Tennis Centre is not even ten minutes drive from where I grew up. It's a plot of green suburban land. The space itself was magic to me. You drove in along a sandy gravel track, past manicured little garden beds and under massive century-old poincianas, planted by Jim's mother.

Jim Joyce talks fast. Really fast. He's funny and direct. And he never stops talking. Even with kids.

I met him for the first time when I was four.

'I don't take them that young,' he told Dad when we arrived.

He believed young children should develop themselves by playing all sports before deciding to do only one thing.

'But I'll take a look at her,' he said, 'and tell you what you can do to practise at home until she's ready in a few years.'

I've always been small, but I must have seemed beyond tiny to Jim that day, standing there with my racquet in hand. I remember its weight and shape even now. Slazenger, 23 inches, green and black. With one string that was broken, repaired and replaced with a single rainbow-coloured thread.

I stood on the service line and Jim tossed me a ball. I sent it whizzing back past his ear.

The next ball Jim picked up was split, so he tossed it to one side of the court as rubbish – but I dashed after it and smacked it too. There was something about that that grabbed Jim. It was my hand–eye coordination and the desperation of the chase.

He looked at me and said, 'You can come back next week.'

Soon tennis was all I could think about. At home was an open carport, under which we loved to play. Young athletes make do with what they have around them, don't they? Dad stuck some masking tape up on the garage wall at the height of a tennis net. I was little, but I hit it against that wall and over that masking tape easily. I served and volleyed. I played points against myself. I had to be forced to come inside. Mostly it didn't bother anyone – except Ali, who would be sitting at the kitchen table doing her homework, hearing that soft *donk, donk, donk.*

I liked that I could imagine where it should go and then make it go there, as if I were controlling something elemental. I became addicted to the creativity. There was magic in it.

I went back to the West Brisbane Tennis Centre a week later, on the Saturday morning after my fifth birthday. Mum made cupcakes to share. And then the lessons began. There were different age groups and different ability levels. The little ones in the morning, before it got too hot. Five courts in total, with about eight kids on any given court. I loved the sound and energy – the pop of a few dozen balls hit, and the laughter from everyone there. Immediately

I wanted to climb each rung. *Gotta get to the next group*, I thought. *Gotta get to the next group.*

Jim picked up on that too, and I progressed through lessons with kids aged six and seven and eight, and soon enough with kids aged nine and ten and 11.

He says my eyes never left him. He would walk and explain, and my eyes tracked him like the pupils in a portrait on the wall. I think I was just being respectful, but he also noticed when we gathered up balls at the end of the session and I balanced half-a-dozen on my racquet, like lemons on a plate. I thought I was just doing what he showed me. He thought of it as a special focus.

There were the fundamentals, of course. Forty minutes of forehands, backhands, slices, volleys, and then – always – 20 minutes of serving at targets. You'd put all the balls in a basket, and serve every one – maybe 70 or 80 balls. Repetition is everything.

Jim found ways to challenge me. He would try to get me to hit a kick serve when I was nine years old, even though no nine-year-old is strong enough to hit one. In a kick serve, the racquet face comes from the back over the top of the ball, giving it topspin.

I found a way to mimic the right technique, but I didn't have the strength to make it hop. When I thought at last I could hit one, Jim would stand about a metre and a half in front of me, facing me, and tell me to serve it over his head. Talk about trust! I was much shorter than Jim, so I had to propel the ball up before it even came down. One day I finally hit one sweetly. 'That kicked!' I said.

Jim just looked at me with a smile. 'But did it? Really?'

He began teaching me the slice backhand too. In many ways, it became the shot that would separate me from other professional women. There's no real trick in the technique. It's nothing more than the extension of a standard backhand volley, hit with enough angle and speed to generate a fade, and an unpredictable low bounce.

In one match, I struggled with my smash. I told Jim I had the yips. He told me to show him, and I hit one sweetly. Bang. He made a few adjustments, but never so many as to overwhelm me.

'Just tilt your shoulder, and adjust your frame,' he said. 'Good, you can smash.'

Later, he told everyone who I played against: 'When she comes to the net, make Ash smash.'

And he told me: 'When you see it up there, you smash it, until that becomes what you do.'

I remember so many of these 'Mr Miyagi moments'.

We would do lessons where I wasn't practising any fundamentals at all – when Jim was just putting the ball in difficult places. I thought we were having fun, breaking up the grind, but really he was teaching me. He knew how to bait me and test me as well as nurse me and praise me.

In so many little ways, Jim was teaching me to play and think differently from everyone else. I came in one day and started making noises when I hit. Just a little grunt or a groan. He asked me if I was sick, and I said no. We went back to hitting and I kept on grunting, so he asked me what I was doing.

'I heard it would give me more power,' I told him sheepishly.

'Asho, that's absolute rubbish,' he replied. 'You do *not* need to grunt. You're not doing any better with it. You're concentrating on grunting instead of hitting. If you grunt again, I'm walking off this court.'

One day I went to practice and was holding the racquet differently.

Jim tilted his head. 'Who are we today?' he asked. Wimbledon was on at the time and I'd been watching Andre Agassi, and I'd decided I should copy his game and even his grip. Jim just sighed, and spent 15 minutes undoing every lesson I'd learned from the TV. But he did it with a smile. 'You're not doing that anymore,' he said.

Jim also found ways to keep me grounded. I played my first competition when I was six going on seven. I was so excited. I'd been practising for almost two years. I was going to win – I was certain of it. Jim made me lose. There aren't many lessons to be learned from an easy win. He found an older girl with the weapons to play me clean off the court.

This philosophy extended to everything I did. Occasionally Jim came along to tournaments. I remember climbing out of my age group, competing when I was 11 against a 14-year-old girl. Jim went to her mother and told her how to beat me. 'Play to her low forehand,' he told them. 'Hit a short slice.'

He knew I would pay more attention to my weaknesses if they led to losses. I won anyway.

One time I won a tournament on the road and got a tall golden trophy, two feet high. I took it into the tennis club to show Jim. I must have been beaming. He held it up, turned it around in his hand, studying it and nodding. Then he walked over to the bin, at the corner of the outdoor court, and dumped it inside.

'That's what that trophy will mean to you down the track,' he said. 'You've got so much further to go.' He smiled then and took it out of the bin again, but the point was made. And at a good time, too.

I began winning quickly, and he kept holding me back from chasing rankings and points. I still won trophies – so many trophies – and he had the idea that we should donate them to less fortunate tennis clubs.

When I was 13, he began lining me up against adult men to force me to find new ways to beat people who were stronger and faster than me. I felt bad for those guys sometimes, as if I was embarrassing them. Jim had to tell me it was okay to win.

After some matches I cried to him, too. I was playing at St Lucia once when I was 12, in a tournament held at the University of Queensland.

Jim had done his usual dirty trick – telling my opponents how to beat me – and one of them did. The tears fell this time. 'I couldn't do it!' I wept to him. 'I couldn't figure her out!'

'It's alright, mate,' he said, giving my shoulder a squeeze. 'You have to learn how to lose.'

There was one girl in particular, Lyann Hoang, who was my best mate and greatest competition. I was forever chasing her, endlessly losing to her power. Jim loved seeing me challenged this way – until I cried again.

'Keep going,' he said. 'One day you'll catch her.'

Finally I did, and I turned to him with a surprised and yet satisfied look.

Jim was as cool as ever. 'Yeah, Asho, but it's just one match. Let's practise again tomorrow.'

I can see why he did it. The ego is a hard thing to keep in check.

We played matches at the tennis centre all the time, testing ourselves against one another. One night

I found myself winning against everyone, no matter how much older, no matter girl or boy.

Jim came walking over, and I was expecting a cool whistle, or even praise, but he just shook his head. 'Your attitude wasn't great. You can't play like that,' he said. 'You have to be able to respect everyone. You can't walk or talk like you're better.'

But such messages take time to sink in. I was playing a match one night after school, and facing off against a boy who was older than me, but who I knew I could beat. We were tied and I was grumpy about this because I thought I should be winning. I was maybe ten years old.

In anger I bounced my racquet, whipping it down onto the concrete surface – and then I heard Jim roar: 'Stop!'

He walked onto the court and pulled me out of there, and instantly I knew I'd screwed up.

'You can't tell Mum and Dad,' I begged. 'They'll yank me out of here by my ear!'

'I know, mate,' he replied. 'But why are you so angry?'

'I should be beating this kid.'

'You never *should* beat anyone.'

'Yeah, but …'

'No. You can't just walk on the court thinking you're gonna wipe the floor with someone. Not with *anyone*. You have to be a better person than that.'

It's easy to see how Jim became part of the family. Mum and Dad trusted him.

Dad agreed with Jim's lesson.

'That's your racquet,' Dad said. 'Just to be clear: if you break it, you're not getting another one.'

'But what am I going to play with?'

'Nothing. You're just not gonna play.'

I didn't need to be told off again. I knew I'd crossed a line. I'm as stubborn and competitive as Dad, but I also want to be the good girl like Mum. I didn't want to get in trouble.

Nothing could keep me away from the West Brisbane Tennis Centre. A tropical thunderstorm might whip through the region, drenching everything and ripping down palm fronds, but Dad would drive me to Jim's anyway, and I would leap out of the car and head straight onto the court. We couldn't run because it was too slippery, but I could still hit volleys and practise my serves. Most important of all, he could still teach me lessons, whether I won or lost.

Black Skin, Red Rocks

Growing up, I knew nothing of the Ngarigo people. Why would I? What would I have in common with an Aboriginal nation from the south – an ancient High Country nation of people whose territory encompassed Jindabyne and Queanbeyan, Canberra and Kiandra, Thredbo and Mount Kosciuszko? Nothing, I would have thought. But I would have been wrong.

I only came to learn what I've learned because of Dad. His skin has that same touch of olive as mine.

When he was little, he thought it was just a tan, just something he got from the long summers spent outdoors. He was 13 when a cousin whispered the real reason to him: their family had Aboriginal ancestry.

Dad asked his parents about this, and they told him a lie. The family had ties to New Zealand, they said, and the Māori warriors across the Tasman Sea. He raised it again later, wanting to know more, and they told him to drop it. He tried again, and this time was sent to his room. It was not a conversation his parents could have with him. To his parents, Aboriginal ancestry was something to be ashamed of.

But Dad was determined, he went on his own journey learning what he could. He unearthed a name, Nancy, his great-grandmother. He pieced together her story, too: how she was married to a white man, and their mixed relationship saw them treated badly in the town.

Dad decided to do something more – to connect with her somehow. He didn't know why exactly or how, but he wanted his heritage confirmed. He was 17 when he finally verified the truth of his family tree. Dad's uncle later found Nancy's grave and headstone on a local property up north, covered in weeds.

Dad told my sisters and me the truth as soon as we were old enough to understand. Sara was 12, Ali ten. I was just seven. I don't remember the news as being a revelation, or even a conversation. I was too little, I guess.

Yet I feel as though I've always known I have Aboriginal ancestry. My favourite picture book growing up was *The Rainbow Serpent*, about the great snake Goorialla, and how in the Dreamtime he used his body to make mountains and gorges and creeks and rivers and a lily lagoon. I remember being transfixed by the tale, from the two brothers seeking shelter and walking into Goorialla's cavernous red mouth, to the men of the tribe finding him coiled and sleeping and cutting open his belly with quartz knives, freeing the brothers, who had now turned into a pair of beautiful rainbow lorikeets. Goorialla woke and raged, of course, and in his fury broke the mountain and threw pieces of it over the land, and all the people fled, and some of them transformed into their totems, brolgas and wombats and kangaroos. Do you remember how it ended? Goorialla disappeared into the sea, and the people who were left knew it was their duty to take care of all the animals – these living things who were once their brothers and sisters. I loved that book, because it was about how our country, creatures, people and plants are all part of the same ancient story.

I was aware of Aboriginal culture in this way, and yet I didn't know then it would change, shape and feed my life going forward.

For Dad, the process of confirming his daughters' ancestry was important. Together, we visited the Kambu Aboriginal and Torres Strait Islander Corporation for Health, a local health centre and hub for helping us to connect with Elders.

Dad helped compile our family history into a long book. He stood in front of the Elders and spoke his truth, and they approved what they heard and read. Our names were recorded as members of the Ngarigo Nation. It was official. We are proud First Nations Australians.

What did all this change for me? At first, not a lot. Perhaps I noticed my world expanding a little bit at school. There were First Nations staff and support workers there who extended a continuous offer of additional help. They also taught us general lessons, about Aboriginal weapons and art and culture.

I came home from school one day with a little didgeridoo and showed Dad.

'That's nice,' he said, 'but you can't play it.'

'Bet I can,' I said.

'No, I mean you're not allowed to play it.'

'What do you mean?'

'Women aren't allowed to play didgeridoo.'

Those are the kinds of things that are only taught to you when you're part of the mob. I learned other things myself, researching online.

The Ngarigo people lived from the Monaro Tablelands to the Bogong High Plains. They were known as 'the moth hunters', because in the warmer months they would begin gathering great masses of bogong moths, and feast on them.

Early accounts describe them as people of the Australian High Country, coming down to the lowlands only for shelter, often sending word in advance through men carrying message sticks to neighbours like the Wolgal and the Yaithmathang, the Theddora and the Biduelli.

They swam in waterholes, where children played in the reeds and men threw boomerangs at drinking birds. They roamed the hills and camped by night and only went to sleep when the moon came out to watch over them.

Their women became famous for the sound of

their 'snow song', a tune sung during corroboree and overheard by a white explorer in 1834, who just couldn't shake the melody. He sketched out the words, then found some friends who could transcribe the musical notes. It became the first piece of published Australian sheet music. The song was only recently 'cleansed' by Ngarigo Elders of its European flavour and restored to what it might have sounded like back then, sung at altitude, under a full moon.

I liked these stories and facts. I liked the way the Ngarigo medicine man is called Murrimalundra, a doctor who extracts the evil substances placed inside sick men. They lived in the most unique environment in Australia, and they knew all its secrets and its science. They knew that mountain celery and that alpine baeckea could be made into medicines.

The Ngarigo people were athletes, too. They played a game with a ball made of possum pelt – women and children running and catching and throwing. It sounds a lot like Marngrook, the original Australian Rules football, the game I love. Few people speak the language now, but a glossary of words exists. A journalist once used that partial dictionary to describe my game. 'Her forehand is like malub, lightning,' he wrote. 'Her smash is like miribi, thunder – her backhand slice like djuran, running water. And she glides lightly on the court like a mugan, a ghost.' I liked the way that sounded.

But I didn't learn any of that until much later. As a kid, I found comfort in the discovery of our ancestry mostly because it helped me understand why I had darker skin and a squishy nose.

Knowing that we were a little different from everyone else, that we were connected to more people throughout the nation gave me a sense of pride. I wanted to walk a little taller. It gave me such joy. That stands in contrast to the sadness I felt for Dad, whose parents could never admit it to themselves or others.

I began reading about the Dreamtime, and storytelling. But there was also something I appreciated that wasn't so much thought as *felt*. Whenever I come home from travelling, I immediately want to be in bare feet, on the grass, sitting in a park, my toes gripping rock or scratching in the dirt. It's what I've always done.

Maybe when I'm doing that I'm feeling a connection to my ancestors, and to the Ngarigo people and to the lands of Bowen, because that sunny place is home, even if the traditional owners in that part of Australia – the Birri and Jangga, Juru, Gia and Ngaro – are not my people.

* * *

I was 14 when I met Evonne Goolagong Cawley for the first time. I had just begun entering junior Grand Slams. My first was the Junior Australian Open in 2011. Evonne came and watched me one afternoon, and after the session Dad introduced me. I remember her sandy linen clothes and long, curly hair, and her lovely big grin. I was shy and wrapped up in a big black hoodie. Evonne said simply, 'I love the way you play,' and gave me a gigantic hug.

I knew who Evonne was, but I didn't know the significance of her life and career – so I started reading about her. I read about a little kid who grew up in a small town. A kid who taught herself to play using a racquet made from a wooden board. Who came to be known as the 'Sunshine super girl'. Who took on the world and won, becoming a seven-time Grand Slam champion, although not without challenges.

Whenever a car came down their road, Evonne's mum would tell her to hide or the welfare man might take her away. Evonne loved music and dancing to disco, and even after she won Wimbledon in 1971, she remembered going out with friends but being turned away at the door because of the colour of her skin.

But she became an inspiration. After that first encounter, we met occasionally on the outdoor courts, at other tournaments or functions or awards nights. I would visit the workshops and events she conducted. And she would reach out to me, to be involved in my life – to observe and enjoy and mentor. It was like she wanted to share my journey, and share what she knew.

Evonne is the kind of person I want to be – someone who gives back, and can use her experiences and profile to encourage others to be their best.

I've seen glimpses and tasted the faintest bitter edge of racism. I'd win a Deadly Award but get vilified online. I'd become a Tennis Australia First Nations Ambassador and then find someone questioning my heritage. I've been lucky to have so many incredible role models. Now I see it as my responsibility to guide First Nations youth and help create opportunities for them to go after their dreams.

I've started by getting involved in clinics in the Red Centre – at a tennis club in Alice Springs, and on a court made of the timeless scarlet sands by Uluru. It was part of the Racquets and Red Dust program to help create sustainable tennis pathways for First Nations people. I was there to promote that, but in all honesty it was seeing the kids smile as they tried something new that got me truly excited.

I was invited on a tour, graciously welcomed to Country by the Anangu people. I listened to our guides as they told stories and explained the significance of the place, the sacred side, the wall art. It was so much bigger and better than I imagined. I wasn't expecting to feel the force of stone – *I have to touch it*, I thought, *I need to*.

I've seen amazing places before, and reacted in all sorts of unexpected ways. The Taj Mahal, the Eiffel Tower, Notre Dame Cathedral, Lord's in 2019 for a cricket World Cup match, the All England Lawn Tennis and Croquet Club where Wimbledon is played.

But that trip to Central Australia was the single most important journey I've ever made. They say Uluru is the heart of the nation. I'm not sure I really believed that until I saw it for myself, and stood in its shadow, feeling the thrum of something ancient inside me, coursing and thumping and echoing through time.

Schoolwork and Broken Hearts

When I was ten years old, a normal week for me might have looked a little abnormal to you. I would come home from school, drop my bag in the middle of the living room floor, ask Mum for some food, go get changed into shorts and a T-shirt, and ask for a lift to Jim's. And that wasn't just most nights, it was *every* night. Monday was fixtures, Tuesday was squad training, Wednesday was a private lesson, Thursday was more squad training and social tennis, Friday was more fixtures, Saturday morning I played idly, and Saturday afternoon was Super League. Sunday I was supposed to have off, but I played anyway. Every single day was tennis.

The only person driving this obsession was me, although the person driving the car was usually Dad. I went on my first road trip with him when I was eight, to Rockhampton where I won the state national title for girls aged ten and under. I won the ladies' trophy in Toowoomba when I was 11 and I won a tournament in Brisbane when I was as small as the ball kids. It seemed as though some youngster had been called up to fill in for an absent player, and stumbled on to a win. I was so small, and so in love with tennis.

We started going on long road trips to Melbourne and Mildura, Bendigo and Bundaberg. We couldn't afford to fly, so we took Dad's latest Ford down the highway, finding cheap places to stay along the way. I got to control the radio, and always put my favourite songs on repeat.

I was the tomboy in our family of daughters, and I grew up alongside Dad on the road. I didn't realise it, but I was learning independence, picking up some new life hack with each stop, about how to clean and pack and take care of myself. I was also getting instructions from Mum on how I needed to look after Dad while we were on the road.

One time we flew to Perth and stayed in a little cabin. I couldn't recall the name of the sauce we used in our stir-fry at home, so I walked up and down the aisles at Woolworths and finally bought a jar of honey and a jar of sweet chilli sauce, which I stirred into our stir-fry that night. Dad smiled as he ate the syrupy dish, and I called Mum, proud of the recipe I'd invented.

It was all an exciting adventure, this strange sporting life. I didn't have a lot of friends to miss, and that was partly due to my personality. I had great friends – I just didn't need a lot of them.

'This is what I'm doing,' I would say to my mates at school. 'If you don't want to do it too, that's fine, but this is the way I'm going.'

I was also spending less time at school anyway. I used to love classwork, and found it easy. I was dux of Grade 8, and my parents expected me to immerse myself in my assignments. On Mum's side of the family, that was simply the rule: you go to school, and then to uni, and then into the workforce. My skipping a few weeks here and there never sat well with her.

Mum was wary of the risks of me aiming at a career in professional tennis. 'It's so hard – you don't know if you're going to make it,' she would say. 'You could make it and get injured. You need something to fall back on.' And yet she also understood that I would never make it as a tennis player unless I put more into the sport than into my studies.

Once, Dad sat me down for a talk. I must have been 12 and we were in a car park. It was 7 am, and

I was eating Weet-Bix out of a plastic bowl before a day full of matches.

He turned to me. 'Do you want to do this?' he asked.

'Do what?' I answered.

'Do you want to try to be a professional tennis player?'

'Yeah, why not? It's what I do.'

'Cool.'

'Cool.'

And that was that.

In Grade 9, we tried distance education. I would go to tennis in Brisbane, and do my schoolwork online. And I hated it. I passed easily but I didn't enjoy their version of school. Classes became an exercise in ticking boxes rather than exploring the world.

Each year my parents and I rethought about what I would learn and when. Would I just study core maths and English? Would I try a TAFE course – maybe a

Certificate IV in Strength and Conditioning? When we were travelling, I'd be sent assignments to complete, but I was too time-poor to do them properly. I got my first C+ in maths in Grade 9 and was devastated, but I was 14 and teaching myself calculus from a textbook. Now, I think a C was actually a good effort.

By the time I reached the senior years of high school, I was attending school maybe 25 days of the year and struggling to keep up. When I was in Year 11 and Ali was at university, I messaged her from a tournament in Malaysia, looking for help with an assignment. She helped me in exchange for more than a few bottles of perfume.

Sara did the same thing to save me in Year 12. Her typical thank-you price was a MIMCO handbag.

There is no way I would have passed without the help of my sisters. We still joke that my high school certificate should also have their names on it.

I didn't attend one day of school in my senior year. I didn't go to my graduation. Or to my formal. In fact,

I often have to ask my mates which year we actually graduated.

Mum was somewhat placated when I found the time for a small-business course at TAFE, and because I read at least a few books every week. And Dad was happy because he thought I was.

In 2011, Dad decided to keep a spreadsheet of how much he and Mum were spending on my tennis. By the time I was 16 it was costing our family $65,000 a year. All of Mum's wage was being poured into travel and gear and tournaments. Sponsors helped, too. HEAD came on board to give me racquets when I was only ten. Adidas took care of my clothes, and eventually FILA. But tennis is an expensive game. You can be among the top 100 players in the world and still have just enough money to live.

Our holidays were no longer at Straddie. A family trip meant my sisters or Mum or Dad would come with me to wherever I was playing, having a 'tennis holiday'. It wasn't much fun for them, and it started feeling that way to me, too.

Tennis Australia had asked if I wanted to be in their national squads when I was ten. But Jim held me back until I was 13 because it means you have to do what Tennis Australia wants. If you want to pick and choose and play your own schedule, then you have to do it without their funding or support.

I went on my first overseas trip – to New Zealand – when I was only 13. Although we had a chaperone, I was used to being with Dad or Mum. I wanted to come home the moment I arrived.

Things were even worse later that year, when I was chosen to join a 'young stars' tour of Europe. The trip was to be seven weeks long. I was younger than all the other kids. Nick Kyrgios was the biggest name there.

We flew to Paris and I tried to be excited. One of the girls showed me how you could watch as many movies as you wanted on the plane, and suggested that I should watch *Taken*, starring Liam Neeson.

'What's it about?' I asked.

'These girls go to Paris,' she said, 'and they get kidnapped.'

'No. I'm not going to watch that movie.'

'Suit yourself.'

I curled up alone in the darkness, already sad and worried, and watched Disney shows to cheer myself up.

I realised quickly that I hadn't packed well. I figured we were just going to play tennis, and I'd brought just one casual T-shirt, for instance. We did a training camp at Roland-Garros and, afterwards, I needed to wash the clay off my gear, but Mum warned me that the industrial washers and dryers at public laundromats might damage my clothes, so while the other kids got out and explored Paris, I sat in a laundromat carefully watching my clothes spin dry. I'm glad I listened to Mum, though, as some of the others burnt holes in their clothes.

We took a bus to the Netherlands next and stayed with other families. My hosts were the Van Poppelins. But the Australian girl I was going to be sharing a room with had to go home after a death in the family, and I didn't know anyone else. I was suddenly alone, too scared to go downstairs and hang with strangers.

The Van Poppelins were concerned, and called Mum. 'Ash goes to her room and won't come down,' they told her. 'She's so sad. What can we do?'

But there was nothing they could do. I was only a few months into my teenage years, by myself, growing up on the road. I called Sara one night when I had bad period pain, not knowing what to do. She told me to run a hot bath, put a towel in it, pull the plastic liner out of the bin and pop the hot towel inside – that would do as a heat pack. I ate my feelings and put on seven kilograms. I cried myself to sleep each night. And then each day I would play.

I won my first round in the Windmill Cup, and in the second round drew the reigning junior European champion, and I beat her too. The other Aussies lost, and prepared to leave.

'But,' I stammered to the organisers, 'you guys can't leave me here …'

'It's okay,' they replied. 'You'll get a bus at the end of the tournament and join us at the next stop.'

'No, you can't leave me here!'

'We're sorry, but we have a schedule to keep.'

I lost 6-4, 6-4 – just close enough that it wouldn't look bad, and I could get on the bus with everyone else.

I was able to talk with Mum and Dad over Skype – it was such a relief to hear their voices. They explained that they never would have sent me if they'd known it would be this way. Still, they couldn't afford to fly over to visit me, nor could they pay for an early flight home. I was stuck.

I still can't believe that was my first experience of the tennis tour. It made me fear travel. For the first time I thought that tennis might not be all I imagined it would be.

When I think of that trip now, it's not something I would ever subject my child or niece or nephew to. The thing I remember most clearly is standing on that court in the Netherlands, crying when I hit a winner and feeling relieved every time I didn't. My dreams of success were getting mixed up with a desire to fail – to get off the court and fly home. That was when I knew I wasn't meant for this life.

The Detroit of Belgium

For almost two years after my 'young stars' Europe tour, I avoided long trips for tennis. I imagined my life lived entirely on the road. Sleeping in hotel rooms. Figuring out foreign food. Talking with family and friends through computer screens, always at strange hours.

Other players enjoy parts of this experience. They find it thrilling to be in a new city every week. I felt no desire to live that way. And so I didn't join another major tour until I was 15.

Again, we went to Europe. I found myself in Belgium, in the city of Charleroi. It has a reputation as the Detroit of Belgium – a city of abandoned buildings and crime.

A year before, I'd played halfway around the world at Nonthaburi, in Thailand, and we had no ground transport, so we walked to and from our hotel. I remember each teen girl walking the humid streets, dodging tuk-tuks with our heavy gear bags on our shoulders, and a racquet always in hand to fend off the feral dogs.

After Charleroi came the clay-court swing in Paris. I won my first-round match at the Junior French Open, before losing in the second. I was playing well enough, I suppose, but struggling all the same. I was homesick.

We went to England next, and I remember the feelings spilling out of me. I wanted to call Dad but I wasn't brave enough, so I sent him a long, sad email.

It was about my misery, but there was one thing I wanted to ask. I needed to start working with a different coach. I needed Jason Stoltenberg.

I first met Stolts in 2007, when he watched me playing as an 11-year-old in the under-12 nationals.

Jim's opinion was very important to me – he and Stolts had hit it off from the start. They had similar styles, and Jim returned to my parents with a message: 'This is the guy.'

Stolts would work with me on a trial basis through the grass-court season.

Now I desperately needed that trial to start, so I hit send on that email to Dad. Stolts was on a plane to England within a few days. I was immediately happy, bubbly, overjoyed to have someone with me who I trusted. Stolts seemed at times like a younger version of Jim. And the way he communicated just made sense to me.

When Stolts arrived, he told me that he'd made the 'Last 8', the semi-finals at Wimbledon, back in 1996.

I told him that was the year I was born – which he didn't like hearing. We at least agreed that 1996 was a good year. But there's an interesting perk of being in the 'Last 8' club at any Grand Slam event: you can forever go back to that event and get free tickets.

'Come on, then,' he said, as my eyes widened. 'Let's see what tickets we can get today.'

We walked into the grandstand, tickets in hand. Our seats were right next to the royal box, and the multiple Grand Slam champion Maria Sharapova was on court warming up. I forget who she was playing against, but it didn't matter. I was buzzing. Stolts knew I needed something to draw me in to the tournament, and experiencing Centre Court on a beautiful summer day was the perfect way to do that.

I confessed to him – 'I've had an average trip'. And he saw it close up in my opening match in the girls' singles. My opponent was 18 and I was 15, so I had a right to be scared. But the pressure I put on myself was too much. I remember standing on

Court 4, before the game had even begun, trying to hide the tears welling up in my eyes.

For me, there was too much foot traffic – too much noise and colour. Too much visibility. Too much attention. My main hope was not to embarrass myself. Somehow, I managed to win.

And I kept winning. I remember one match well, against someone who would one day become a constant rival: Madison Keys. She was in the top five juniors in the world at this point, but I had more than a hunch I could beat her.

'I *know* she can't hit a forehand down the line – I saw it last week,' I said to Stolts. 'She can't hit it. All I have to do is force her to hit that forehand down the line.'

In the end, I put the ball where it needed to be, and she pulled the trigger. Missed by a country mile.

Stolts just smiled and shook his head.

After winning five matches, I was into the final. This was different: it was played on Court 1, where the grandstand holds 7500 people, and it was full. I've never felt physically ill walking out on court before, but I did then. I was playing against a Russian lefty named Irina Khromacheva, and I wanted to vomit.

I walked down the tunnel into the arena, past all the pictures of former champions, and I tripped and stumbled on the carpet. It was only as I walked into the light and sound of the court that I realised … This. Is. So. Cool.

The travel and the isolation will never be enjoyable, but even when that becomes a struggle, an athlete never feels so comfortable as they do in the game itself. This is what we train for.

I won the final 7-5, 7-6, ending it with a forehand cross-court winner and a tiny little fist-pump. I was handed the trophy and told to do a victory lap.

'I can't walk a lap parading this trophy,' I said. 'My opponent is right there!'

'You have to,' they whispered. 'Present the trophy, clap and walk slowly past the photographers.'

With the trophy in my hands, I was uncomfortable. Everyone was looking at me, and I didn't like that. They asked me to kiss the trophy too. 'Go on! Do it! Give it a kiss!'

But again I couldn't.

'You have to!'

I had promised myself I would only ever kiss a Grand Slam trophy, and nothing else. I kept my promise.

The media circus began. Two hours of talking – not just at a press conference but in one-on-ones with local reporters, and reporters from Australia and from Russia.

I had my first experience with a doping test, too. A chaperone walked into a bathroom with me, to watch me pee in a cup. I couldn't go, and the lady was unimpressed.

'You need to go,' she said.

It took me four hours to produce a sample. It was all so confronting that already I was wishing I'd lost.

'There's one more thing,' Stolts told me. 'There's a winners' ball tonight and you have to go.'

'Sorry, I can't,' I replied. 'My flight home is waiting.' I had already changed my flight home once and was booked to depart that night.

He kept making the case: I had to go. The champions always go. An Australian boy, Luke Saville, had won the final of the boys' tournament, so I could go with him. The professional champions would be there: Novak Djokovic and Petra Kvitová. The event would be fun.

'I can't change this flight again,' I declared. 'I have to go home.'

That was when Dad called me, and when I answered I didn't give him the chance to speak. 'I can't go to this ball tonight,' I blurted out. 'I'm not changing my flight.'

'First of all, Ash, congratulations,' he said, warmly. 'And, darl, you have to go.'

'I can't go, and I'm not going,' I repeated. 'I've been away for six weeks. I'm coming home.'

I knew some people would love to go to such a ball. I thought about how they would love to get dressed up to the nines, and walk the famous purple carpet into a ballroom. Others would attend out of a sense of obligation or tradition. I did neither. It was the first time a champion has ever skipped the ball.

I went to take a shower instead, and calmed myself down, thinking only of home. I didn't have to go back to my hotel for my things, because I was already packed. I caught a Wimbledon car alone to the airport, boarded my flight, curled up in my seat and slept the entire way home. I awoke in Brisbane to cameras everywhere. They had already been to Dad's work at the State Library, and Mum's work at the hospital – and now they were here to get a photo of me hugging my family at arrivals. They were there to capture the moment – and 'capture' feels like the right word. They stole it from us – locking it up in film and making it their own. I just wanted to give Mum and Dad a hug.

Arriving home as a champion suddenly felt disappointing. The response to my victory showed me a truth. *This is not tennis*, I thought to myself. *This is something else.*

Stolts knew it too. He made a point of debriefing with Mum and Dad later – telling them of my wonder at Centre Court, my stumbles and tears on Court 4, my refusal of all ceremony after the win.

'Ash could do brilliant things,' he told them. 'But it's gonna be tough. And we'll need to be very careful.'

Good Habits

Training with Stolts was so much fun. He knew to allow me to work on the slice and the chip and the drop shot. We would do drills where he would ask me to hit a different shot on every ball. He never wanted to stop my creativity. For Stolts, it was about letting me know that it was safe to play the way I liked to play.

'Let's never hit the same ball twice in a row,' he suggested.

He kept the sessions short, too. Quality over quantity. But he also corrected my faults and flaws.

At 15, I wasn't moving my feet nearly enough. A tennis player needs to always be moving. I wasn't doing that. I was standing still but I was getting away with it.

If I wanted to get even better, Stolts said, I needed to be on my toes more, thinking with the balls of my feet. Good habits, he called it – I should start to build the good habits.

Stolts believed that my style was inherently *mine*. He taught me to use my strengths and build the rest of my game around them, because that's how he learned, too.

Jason Stoltenberg grew up in the country, in northern New South Wales, on a vast property an hour from town. The sign on the way says, 'Australia's greatest sporting town', in large part because Stolts and a few others were born or started their careers there.

Stolts was eight when he picked up a racquet to compete in a tennis day being held in town, and he won, so his family decided to build a court on a paddock near their house.

He left home for Sydney at 14 and went to the Australian Institute of Sport (AIS) in Canberra next, as part of a strong squad. He was lucky to find coaches there who allowed him to play his game. He developed his own feel for tennis, and it shaped the way he would one day teach.

He became a real good player, too. In 1987, he won the boys' singles title at the Australian Open, and was the number 1 ranked junior player in the world. His career-high ranking was 19 in the world, and he stayed in the top 100 for over ten years.

Stolts' first job in coaching was with Lleyton Hewitt, who had just become number 1 in the world. Stolts loved finding ways to get the very best out of people, but it came at a cost. During the first year he was on the road for 41 weeks, and it forced him to ask a question: 'Am I going to be a father or a coach?'

I love that he asked that question of himself. He left behind the global tour and worked in local development and coached juniors from a court in his backyard.

I began working with him at 15, the week before Junior Wimbledon, and then I moved by myself to Melbourne – so I could train under his guidance. It was winter, and I'd never felt so cold or alone.

I had no idea how to live alone. Mum had prepared a binder with all my favourite family recipes: from spaghetti bolognese to beef stir-fry with fried rice, and even step-by-step instructions on how to make a simple chicken wrap. I wanted it to taste just like it did at home.

It was also the first time I'd ever gone into a hard, professional training block. I enjoyed that I was doing something at the highest level – being tested and challenged, getting home tired and waking up sore, and doing it all again the next day.

I was hardening up, building my body and making it susceptible to stress. Walking lunges. Lateral jumps. Running with resistance. Planking with resistance. Weights. Boxing. Sprinting from side to side on the court, and tipping my racquet head down like a batter touching the crease between runs. Stolts organised for me to hit with men who were playing big-time tennis – guys who knew how to hit monster forehands that would test out a teenage girl, but who would not get rattled if they lost a few points to her too.

Stolts was assessing my tennis but also my mood and motivation. He was trying his best to truly *see* me. But I was a 15-year-old girl and was already adept at hiding my fears and keeping quiet. I came out of that training block a better tennis player, yet still fragile.

Stolts, Dad and I went to the United States, where I was ranked the number 2 junior in the world. In a warm-up tournament before the US Open, I lost my first-round clash to a Canadian wildcard, and I cried.

'It's alright,' said Stolts, somewhat confused. 'We've only trained for six weeks. It'll take time.'

At the US Open itself, I found a way to win some tough matches. I made it to the semi-finals but lost, and again I wept. My explanation sounds ridiculous now, but I cried and cried and tried to explain why.

'I've failed,' I said. 'I didn't win.' I was like a six-year-old, still needing to be told that I couldn't win all the time.

Stolts was worried. He could sense my struggles. People looking in from the outside must have thought everything was great – but Stolts knew better.

Wildcards

By early 2012 I was still only 15, but now I was playing and winning in the under-18s at nationals. Apparently, that made me the only person in Australian history to have won the national title in under-12s, under-14s, under-16s and under-18s by the age of 15. When I heard that, I could feel that old familiar pressure building once more.

Next, I was entered into the wildcard playoffs for the 2012 Australian Open. It's a tournament where 16 Aussies who sit outside the top 100 compete for one spot in the Grand Slam event.

In my first match I faced Casey Dellacqua. The woman who would later become my dear friend was 26 at the time, a full 11 years older than me, and even though she was managing injuries, she was experienced. She had a spot in the singles draw of the Australian Open in her sights, but I beat her. I went on to win our pool, and then I continued winning my way through to the final, where I beat Olivia Rogowska in the biggest match of my young professional career. And that was that: I had earned a place in the Australian Open – my first ever Grand Slam event.

In the first round I drew Anna Tatishvili, who was among the top 50 players in the world at that time. Can you imagine being ranked that highly at what you do? Anna Tatishvili won with ease.

I had at least been part of the main competition, as a young and still slightly built teenager, and my ability was clearly growing.

So, I took my first steps out of junior competition and into professional play. I played tournaments that were close to home. The first was in Sydney – an event that I went on to win. I won another a week later, on grass in Victoria. I compiled a singles record that season of 34 wins and just four losses across nine tournaments. Stolts tried his best to keep my progress steady, but I kept on winning and my improvement kept accelerating. I wasn't being overworked, either – I simply got better through natural growth.

The pressure began throbbing again, too. I feared failure: *What if I don't achieve these things that people think I should?* But I also feared success: *What if I do well enough that this lonely way of living becomes my life?* I was trapped in the game.

I also started playing doubles with Casey and began winning there, too. We began crashing our way into doubles finals all over. I was only 16 when we made the final of the 2013 Australian Open, the first

Aussie duo to reach the women's doubles final since Evonne Goolagong Cawley and Helen Gourlay in 1977. We made the final at Wimbledon and the US Open, too. We won the Birmingham Classic on grass and the Internationaux de Strasbourg on clay. But doubles wasn't the reason I played – singles was – and in singles I was struggling.

I was 16. I wasn't exactly a child anymore. All my life I'd been told I was a prodigy: 'You're gonna be the next big thing' and 'You'll be world number one someday.' And I had started to believe it. That scared me – what were all those people who put me on a pedestal going to think if I failed?

'Watch this girl,' they used to say, 'she's going places.' And the people listening would sagely nod and murmur their own endorsements.

'Nothing surer,' they would confirm. 'She's the next Martina Hingis.' But Martina Hingis won the Australian Open when she was 16 years and 117 days old, the age I reached halfway through 2013.

I knew I wasn't being fair on myself – I couldn't seriously expect to perform as well as the youngest Grand Slam winner in the history of tennis. That's not a standard anyone should force themselves to meet. But it didn't matter how logically I looked at things. I felt like a failure.

I didn't know how to name these issues either. I did know a little bit about depression, through my dad, who has suffered from this through his life. I could always tell the difference between those times when Dad was taking his medication and when he was taking a break from them. I knew he had found his right balance, with the help of my Aunty Robyn, an extraordinary doctor. Now I wondered if perhaps I needed to do the same thing.

I was at an ITF event in Birmingham, Alabama, when I took action. I was sitting on a grassy hill above a green clay court when I fired off a Facebook message: *Aunty Rob – are you available to chat?* I almost hoped she wouldn't reply, but she did.

She wanted to know more, and so I told her, crying as I typed. I didn't know how to tell her what I was feeling. *I just know I'm sad*, I wrote. *And I don't know why.*

That was the start of my therapy. It was my way of being brave enough, not face to face (yet) or by phone (yet), but by brief messages and long emails. I trusted Aunty Rob, loved her, and she helped me unravel my situation.

She helped me recognise the way my mood would plummet in the weeks before any tour. We tried different medications, different conversations, and eventually we found the right blend and I started to feel more stable. My emotions began to level out. I began opening up and talking more to my family and friends about how I was feeling – the people I knew I could lean on, but was never courageous enough to. Aunty Robyn helped me understand why I was feeling the way I was.

I don't have to do what I'm doing, I began to think. *I have a choice.*

But identifying your problems isn't the same thing as getting rid of them. I was still a kid. I had enough issues just being a girl in the world.

I had massive worries about my body, which developed when I was around 13. When away from home, I had no awareness or routine, and therefore no normal routine for meals, so I over-ate. I didn't know how to navigate different foods in Europe, where the traditional breakfasts were bread and pastry. I would put on weight by comfort eating, too, before going to bed. Do you know how many different flavours there are in the Milka chocolate range? More than you can imagine.

And when I wasn't putting on kilograms through my middle, I was gaining functional weight elsewhere. I'm built like an athlete. So, I would train and play and eat and sleep and my quadriceps would explode. You need that strength as a tennis player because you rely on your legs for every single shot. Every part of your movement is driven by the power in your legs and the strength of your core. But I hated the way the training showed.

I couldn't celebrate being unique because I was too worried about being seen to be different.

I didn't tell anyone how I felt sharing a locker room with women who had trained their entire lives to be lean and long and strong – gifted and beautiful goddesses from South America and Eastern Europe. I didn't tell anyone about how they would walk around without a towel on and I wouldn't know where to look, only that I didn't want anyone seeing me so exposed. I got changed in a shower cubicle each day.

By the time 2014 rolled around and I was 17 years old, none of those feelings had been shaken. Naturally, that was the year of my first-round match at the Australian Open against the great Serena Williams.

I've never felt so intimidated. We stood on the court and I felt as though I was beaten before the match even began. I knew my Australian Open was over the day her name was drawn against me. She wore her ponytail up high – I remember the way it magnified her presence – and turned her shoulders over and over during the warm-up, a picture of perfect prowling menace. I went into that match hoping to last an hour, but the 6-2, 6-1 rout took only 57 minutes. Again, I experienced that feeling of failure.

Looking back, I just wish I had been more courageous in that match. I wish I had given myself a chance.

I wish I'd known that bravery isn't always something you're born with: it can also be something you learn. I wish I knew then what I know now.

Big, Ugly Tears

Something was building. It was the middle of winter in 2014, and I found my mood going all over the place. I would be hypersensitive and then numb, disciplined and then lazy. Mainly, though, I think I was longing for the normal life I always thought I could live – a life that was now clearly out of reach.

In one of the cooler months down in Melbourne, I flew north to a family gathering – one of those big get-togethers where there were dozens of us enjoying one another's company.

It made me imagine children of my own. I pictured holidays on Straddie where they would learn to fish, just as I had done. I could teach them how to tuck little bags of worms into their togs and how to balance while holding a rod on the rocks by the shoreline. I could ground them – and myself – in an ordinary life.

Instead, I was spiralling through a different universe entirely, like some alien child. What teenager travels the world alone for a living, sleeping in an interstate apartment, making her own meals and exercising daily in some cold, faraway city?

I remember I was training one day in Melbourne, and I was suddenly fed up. That makes me sound defiant, but in reality I sat crying alone on the changing room floor at the National Tennis Centre.

I knew I was done in that moment. I made up my mind to quit, but I didn't yet have the courage to let it be known.

Instead, I texted Stolts. *I can't train tomorrow*, I wrote. *I feel sick*.

In truth, I just wanted to go to the 18th birthday of a mate, so I flew to Queensland and did exactly that. I felt as though missing that party would have been awful in some way. It was as though this one party for a bunch of teenage mates had become symbolic of all the normal things I'd given up. Out on the town in Brisbane, I immediately felt like I could breathe again.

There, my decision became real. *Professional tennis is not for me*, I thought. *I want to do something different.*

Days later, back in Melbourne, I asked Stolts if we could talk. We sat on a couch in a large open area on the third floor of the National Tennis Centre.

I looked up at him with a tremble in my lip, but I couldn't hold his eye. 'I think I want to stop,' I whispered. 'I can't do this anymore.'

Stolts was silent but looked right into my eyes, offering a gentle, encouraging look. He said nothing, but if his expression could have spoken it would have warmly said two words: *Go on.*

'I'm not enjoying it,' I continued. 'I need to step away ... and stop playing.'

He wasn't surprised or upset. He didn't offer alternatives or seek details. He just nodded and smiled. 'Ash, I know,' he said. 'I get it. And it's okay.'

I looked back at him, eyes wet.

'It's no problem,' Stolts continued. 'It's fine. You need to disconnect. It's the right thing to do.'

He sat next to me and put his arm around me, and with that I had a big, ugly cry, and the weight of the world slipped from my shoulders.

'I'm proud of you,' he said. 'I'm proud of your decision.'

I played one last tournament: the US Open in September 2014. I didn't want to let Casey down in the doubles.

I didn't quite know how to tell everyone else, but none of them were surprised. It was clear to them all already that I was suffering from depression. I'd been quiet for weeks, speaking to almost no one. That's unlike me: when I'm comfortable, I'm the clown of the family.

I made my family aware one by one, on the phone or in person, tearing the bandaid off slowly. I couldn't bring myself to tell Mum and Dad until they dropped me off at the airport. My last words before saying goodbye: 'This is going to be my last tournament.'

I played terribly, of course. There were no flashes of brilliance to make me reconsider. There was no movie moment in which I played a point and hit a ball square in the middle and heard that rich sound of something struck perfectly and decided that I couldn't give up this game I knew so well and loved so much.

I lost my first-round singles match to Barbora Záhlavová-Strýcová 6-1, 6-3, and Casey and I lost our first-round doubles match to Gabriela Dabrowski and Alicja Rosolska 6-2, 6-3.

Straight sets. Both times. Going, going, gone. I headed to John F. Kennedy International Airport and boarded a plane with a high school certificate, no job and no idea what I was going to do with my life. I flew home smiling, as if drifting on a cloud.

* * *

And then ... normal life restarted. A regular teenage life. I lived back at home with Mum and Dad, helping Mum in the garden and taking out the bins every Thursday. I began hanging out with my mates on weekends. I watched Test matches at the Gabba. I went camping in the Scenic Rim, outside the city. I wasn't bored but I wasn't stimulated, and that was actually ideal. For a while.

Cricket found me in 2015. The Women's Big Bash League (WBBL) was about to start, with the aim of becoming a major domestic women's sporting competition. I knew the physio of the Australian women's cricket team and she gave me a call.

'They're looking for a few different athletes,' she said. 'Would you be keen?'

Cricket was, in a way, my first sporting love – the game I watched more than any other. When I was a ten-year-old girl in 2005, I didn't stay up overnight watching the French Open – I stayed up watching Shane Warne play the cricket of his life in a losing Ashes series.

But I had never played cricket, other than in the backyard and the driveway. I'd never owned my own bat, or worn pads. And yet I found myself at cricket training one Saturday morning at Allan Border Field in Albion, ready to practise with the Queensland state team. I didn't know what to take, so I slung a Country Road bag over my shoulder with a water bottle and some sunscreen inside.

I arrived for a loose warm-up – I was mainly a spectator, there to watch and listen. I had never seen women's cricket up close before, and I marvelled at the players' skill level. The technique was sound, they bowled faster than I imagined was possible, and the way they could use the willow to crush those deliveries – wow.

Then it was my turn to have a net, and I faced up to an automated bowling machine. Andy Richards, the head coach, chucked me a bat and some pads from his kit bag. He asked about a helmet.

'Nah, mate, I think I'll be okay,' I said. I'd never worn one in my life – never needed to. With all the girls watching on, I punched a hard cover drive off my first delivery and felt the ball rocket off the centre of the bat. I missed a few, too, but I had fun.

I'd thought it was a meaningless casual session, but found out later that I'd actually been auditioning for a spot with the WBBL club Brisbane Heat. And they wanted me.

Delissa Kimmince was the captain at the time, and she took me under her wing, quickly making it clear that no one was fazed by my tennis career.

'Are you gonna keep bringing that Country Road thing,' she asked me the following week, 'or get yourself an actual cricket bag?'

In little ways like this, my new teammates gave me a hard time, and I gave it right back to them. I loved it. I fitted in without having to change myself at all, and was soon doing three sessions a week, as well as playing locally on weekends.

Mum came along to watch my very first intraclub practice game before our season started. Australian spinner Jess Jonassen – one of the best bowlers in the world – was at the other end of the pitch. She crept in to bowl and knocked me over for a duck. Mum had come along to support me, and had watched with glassy-eyed boredom as I stood in the field all day – only to see me go out first delivery. A day's worth of work undone with a single bad stroke.

I did better next game, scoring 63 runs off 60 balls and taking two wickets bowling gentle (very gentle) offies, and then I settled in for a full summer season. I played well. I'll never forget the first century I made, at our home ground in Graceville. I called Dad immediately after coming off the field.

'Dad, I made a century!'

He laughed down the phone line. 'You're ridiculous,' he said, 'but I love you.'

I spotted Mum on the drive home, while she was out walking the dogs. 'Mum!' I screamed from the car window, 'I made a hundred!' – and she nearly fell over, I gave her such a start.

I enjoyed playing for the Westies, and never more so than in our Grand Final. I was our top scorer that day with 37 runs, but I couldn't have cared less about my performance so much as winning as part of a group. I remember being roasted in the sun and then cracking open cool drinks in the sheds, celebrating together and thinking, *How good is this?*

By now I had signed on with the Brisbane Heat for the inaugural season of the Women's Big Bash League, and I was lucky enough to play in the first ever WBBL match. There was real excitement building among the girls who had waited so long for rightful recognition on the national stage.

They approached the sport with such love for each other. I loved that element of the game. I loved the fact that even if I lost – failing as an individual – the team could still win.

And yet, in another way, I didn't like that at all. I missed the accountability – the sense that my errors are my errors, my decisions are my decisions, and they have consequences for me. I missed the one-on-one competition of tennis.

I began coaching tennis with Jim back at the beautiful old West Brisbane Tennis Centre, under the jacarandas and poincianas.

Jim was happy to have me, because I was happy to do everything, working mornings and afternoons and nights across all five courts. I would take charge of junior fixture competitions, teaching little kids how to score the game. I did group lessons for promising teenagers. I did private lessons for little old ladies playing socially. Jim had a school tennis program, and would send me out to run them.

Jim joked with me about how he'd given me the boring jobs he didn't want to do. He hoped I would grow tired of coaching and realise I was made to play, but I loved it all.

I even tolerated Jim's jokes about cricket. He'd tease me after I'd spent an entire weekend baking in the field before losing my wicket cheaply.

'That must have been fun,' he would say, smirking. 'Compare that to playing Serena Williams at the Australian Open.'

And, slowly but surely, without even realising it was happening, I found myself with a nagging itch.

Part of me knew that I had left tennis without

ever fully investing in it and giving the game my all – I had always held something back.

Now I felt guilty and curious – not about how many tournaments I might have won, but where tennis might have taken me. *Maybe*, I thought, *I owe it to myself to find out.*

A B C D

There's a story people tell about me, about my comeback to tennis. The short version is that Casey Dellacqua, my best mate and doubles partner, brought me back to tennis with a casual hit one day.

It's true, at least in a basic sense. But it's also important to know that Case wasn't trying to get me back into the sport. In fact, she was easing herself back into tennis. She was overcoming an awful injury.

I should zoom back first, though, to when Case and I met. I was just 13, little more than a scared kid, and she was 24, an already fierce competitor on court. I texted her at the time to ask if she would play doubles with me at the Brisbane International, as a wildcard entry. It was a risk for Case, yet she took a chance on me. I was just a kid and she was already a well-established doubles player. But we clicked from the get-go.

She loved my tennis. She told me what impressed her was my court sense – that spatial awareness that allows you to cover the right parts of the playing surface. Tennis is definitely about the choices you make – the shots you take and the places you run – as well as the skills and fitness you build.

We took the time to learn and love each other's stories. Case had never really been a top junior. She had to fight her way through. She grew up in Perth, far removed from the southeastern centre of tennis in this country, and she moved to the Australian Institute of Sport in Melbourne alone when she was 16. She struggled with that just as I had. She reached the top 100 by the time she was 20.

Case was a decade older yet made me feel like a peer, a friend – someone I was going to have fun with on court. She's the most childlike, caring, fun-loving person ever. As I was introduced to the tour, Case became my sister, my mum, my *person* when we were on the road.

We became a perfect partnership. Our games complemented each other's. Case gave me the belief and permission on court to be creative and have fun. She plays on first court, on the deuce side, and has one of the best cross-court backhands in the game while I love to hit my forehand inside out, and chip around with a backhand slice. So her strengths covered my weaknesses, and vice versa, and we became a deadly lefty-righty combination.

ABCD. Ash. Barty. Casey. Dellacqua.

The doubles competition often gets passed over in tennis. Do our minds ever turn to the pairs? Martina Navratilova and Pam Shriver won 21 major doubles titles – 21! – including the 'Golden Slam' in 1984, but do we even recall that they competed together for so long? And what of those doubles specialists, such as the Bryan brothers, Bob and Mike, who never competed highly in singles but have together won more doubles titles than any other pair. How many exactly? One hundred and twelve!

Overall, doubles is often dismissed or even forgotten.

In October 2015, Case was playing doubles with Yaroslava Shvedova at the China Open. She turned to get up for a smash but tripped and fell and hit her head on the hard court. Case doesn't remember the final minutes of the match at all, but was told later that she walked off the court and vomited immediately then woke up in a Beijing hospital.

She had suffered a horrific concussion. She couldn't walk in the light. Headaches were constant. Normally she was outgoing and bubbly; now a quiet anxiety began to boil inside her. Case didn't want to talk to anyone or go anywhere or do anything.

She never played another singles match, and thought she would never play again at all.

That's where her life was at in early 2016. And me? I was about to head to Sydney for a cricket game. That was when she texted me.

Yo bra when do u get in? Is it tomorrow or Thursday? Are u bringing ur racquets?

Yo tomorrow! 10 am I think I land. Yeah I'll bring a couple of racquets down, chuck them in with my cricket kit. Gotta bring it all down with me.

Yah cool mate. I will come & get u from airport just text me when u land & I'll meet u in the pick-up spot. Would you be keen for a hit tomorrow arvie & then watch a bit of tennis at Homebush? Excited to see ya!!

Oh, you're a legend. Yeah, I'll have a bash. Not sure if it'll be any good. I'll come out for sure, no worries.

Haha, don't worry, I'm only a few hits in so I'm rusty. We can just have a quick fun bash yah cool.

We walked into Homebush together while the Sydney International was being played. We picked a quiet time to go out on one of the courts when no one was around.

And then straightaway, first hit, first ball: *Ohhh, I thought. I've missed this.*

It was the slice backhand that got me: hook, line and sinker. We hit some more and had a few laughs and screwed around, and I realised I'd forgotten how much I loved doing that together. We were both self-conscious, of course. *Is Case making a comeback? Am I? Or are we just two friends hitting balls to one another?* All I could think about was how much joy I felt.

And I'd forgotten how easy it is to fall into a rhythm with the person on the other side of the net, whether it's your coach or hitting partner or opponent. Have you ever not seen a friend in ages – maybe months or even years have gone by without contact – and you're nervous about seeing them again, and all those nerves go away because you slide back into your relationship as though you'd never stopped talking in the first place? In the fading afternoon light that day, with the last of the sunset casting across the court, tennis suddenly felt like that.

It helped that it was Case. We needed each other, and we needed the game that had brought us together. We hit and hit and I messed up a few but went through the whole range, and we sweated and laughed and stretched.

What am I doing out here? I wondered. *Why are we not on court together, playing in this tournament?*

We went back to Case's for a BBQ, and that evening I called Stolts. I think when he saw his phone ring, he knew exactly what the call was about.

My decision was made. I was returning to tennis.

When I told my family, they simply nodded as though they'd seen this coming. Jim definitely knew, after we met and chatted for hours one day. We mainly talked about how to plan my return.

'Jimbo, I reckon this is what I'm meant to do,' I told him.

He agreed, with no 'told you so' – just a nod and a wink. He had a few ideas about what Ash Barty 2.0 might look like: how I would need to embrace everything and make this second phase of my career utterly my own. Choose my own team. Choose my own tournaments. Book my own flights. Make decisions for myself. I wanted that accountability.

'This time around, do it your way,' he said. 'Do it *all* your way. Keep the ball in your court.'

Faster, Flatter

In February 2016 – with my P-plates on – I took my car, named Frankie, on a road trip. I'd bought Frankie a few years back when I was 17 as a gift to myself when Case and I made the doubles final at Wimbledon.

In my 2016 road trip I took Frankie down the coast through Byron Bay and Coffs Harbour and Taree, Newcastle and Sydney and Albury, headed for Melbourne. Specifically, I was headed for the headquarters of Tennis Australia, to chat with CEO Craig Tiley about starting up my career from scratch, utterly unranked.

Before I could get in to see the TA boss, I spied a guy sitting at his desk looking not particularly busy. His name was Craig Tyzzer.

I had worked briefly with Tyzz back in 2012 and 2013. Stolts had asked him to come on a couple of different trips to give me some tactical instruction. I remembered that he was always practical, grounded in reality and never tied to emotion. He had a way of breaking down opponents and helping me walk around their weaknesses.

Tyzz came to the tennis world via the scenic route.

He grew up in Oak Park, a housing development area north of Melbourne. He played footy and cricket growing up, and tennis later, when the local council built some tennis courts virtually in his backyard.

Eventually, Tyzz played on tour, for a few years anyway. He struggled to maintain a presence on tour, though, because of a lack of funding. He also badly injured his shoulder, and it became a choice between an operation or rest. He couldn't really afford to do either.

As his playing career faded, Tyzz began doing some junior coaching. He learned care and trust, and how to work with individuals. Tyzz had been raised on a 'one size fits all' approach to coaching – if you didn't cut the mustard, there was something wrong with you – and now he was learning about the opposite. Coaching went from something he never thought he would do to the only thing he would consider doing.

His brother Roger was head of the Competitive Edge program in Texas. Tyzz joined him there running tennis academies, tennis vacations, tennis camps and *fantasy* tennis camps. The tagline: 'You take the best from down under, blend it with Texas flavor, and put it in the middle of the Hill Country. We call it "Aus-Tex" hospitality. You won't find that anywhere, mate!'

The main purpose, Tyzz told me once, was to get talented kids into college on tennis scholarships. And they were incredibly successful. Tyzz stayed until he had experienced just enough of America and then decided to come home. He landed at a local Melbourne club, coaching players while also working at schools.

The first professional he worked with was Andrew Ilie. Ilie had been injured, and was desperate to return to his best. They started together from scratch, working with new doctors. Tyzz worked on changing his serve to overcome a troublesome back. Ilie never reached great heights but became a kind of cult figure, a fan favourite for his outrageous shots and outlandish celebrations, including a tradition of tearing his shirt after memorable wins. Together, they made it to number 38 in the world. Again, it's worth remembering what that means. The idea that there are 193 countries and 7.7 billion people on the planet, and yet there are only 37 people out there better than you at what you do? That's incredible!

Stolts played against Ilie quite often, so he got to know Tyzz too. That's why I knew Tyzz well enough to say hello to him that day in February 2016 at Tennis Australia. I stopped to say g'day, wondering why he was at his desk at 10.30 in the morning. Apparently, he had just finished up working with Daria Gavrilova, and was without an athlete. I was without a coach. They say timing is everything …

'Huh,' I said, thinking for a moment. 'You want to come out and hit a few balls?'

'Sure,' he replied. 'What are you doing here, anyway?'

'I'm gonna play a small doubles event in Perth in a few weeks. Do you maybe want to do some work with me?'

'Yeah, okay.'

We found a court, and hit and chatted, and laughed at the rusty hinges of my swing. Tyzz worked through all my shots and then shot me a look. 'How long has it been since you hit?' he asked.

'Yeah, yeah,' I acknowledged. 'Ease up. It's been a while.'

Then we talked about what I was doing and how I was feeling.

'This time, I wanna do it my way,' I said. 'I want to make my own decisions. I want to pick the travel I do, and pick the tournaments that matter. I want time off when I need it. I want to choose the team around me.'

'I like it,' Tyzz said. 'In fact, I love it.'

I also needed to know what he saw in me – and I didn't mean the stuff he'd seen me do well. Tyzz is able to pick people apart and find their flaws. What did he think I needed to improve?

Tyzz said I had more than a few areas for growth. 'You have to work on your serve,' he explained. 'You have to be taller.'

That might sound strange, as you can only be as big as you are. But it means using everything you can to get *up* to the ball. The higher you are, the more space you have to clear the net.

'You're not exactly tall,' Tyzz said. 'So you need drive to strike the ball higher.'

I also needed to work on my accuracy and placement. The serve is the one shot in tennis that is in your full control. I wanted to do everything possible to make it a weapon.

There's even a psychological aspect. If your serve becomes reliable, your opponents will get nervous because of it.

My backhand needed plenty of work too. The slice backhand was always good – no need to tinker too much with that technique – but Tyzz had a question about my positioning. There are subtle differences in the set-up for a two-handed backhand and a slice backhand. It can be a delicate balance, but also a movement that you can be aggressive with. The tricky part is moving your feet fast enough, so that you switch between the double-hander and the slice. If you can master that, you can play the single-handed slice backhand more often.

'And that's a weapon,' Tyzz said. 'Nobody else plays it, so a lot of girls will just lose their marbles as soon as they see it.'

Picking the right ball to hit the slice is crucial too. With a lower and faster ball, I often chose to hit the slice, because I can get underneath it and use its pace. With a wider and slower ball, we worked on hitting the two-hander, because you have to get your body behind it and generate your own power and speed.

We also needed to work on perfecting different *kinds* of slices, Tyzz said. To really master the art. A faster, flatter slice. A spinny slice. A slow slice. A slice that floats and pops. Aggressive slice, defensive slice. No one will spot the variety because the adjustment is so subtle, so if you can perform each variant, you can wrong-foot your opponent with every strike.

We started a training block that would take us through March, April, May and part of June, and during that time I got to know Tyzz better. He is astute. He's also a clown. He's emotionally intelligent. He's focused. He surfs to clear his mind.

But before I could trust this man and put his training into practice, he had a little bad news for me. There was one thing I needed before we could begin.

'It's fitness,' Tyzz said. 'We need to make sure you're 100 per cent fit, and able to stand up to the training. We need to get you into shape – because right now, Ash, you're not.'

The Wolves of Wimbledon

Tennis asks questions of you and the biggest question of all is: *In a sport with lots of injuries – including one nicknamed after it (the tennis elbow) – can my body handle the physical pressure?*

That first year back in the game, the answer was no. I kept getting injured. My recurring problem was humeral bone stress, which affects the bone in the upper arm. My right arm was not coping with the increase of pressure and impact, with the muscles pulling around that bone. It was getting more and more sore. Partly that's due to the way I play and the strings I use. The co-polyester string I prefer gives me power, control and touch, but it is still a hard string, and it takes time and strength to be able to withstand the brutal impact of my training loads.

In the early days with Tyzz, I had to train and then rest, train and then rest. We did 40 weeks of training in that first year alone and I suffered four injury setbacks in that time, mostly due to the actions I had to do over and over again. Luckily, we had help – the very best. Strength and conditioning coach Narelle Sibte – a Melbourne girl who calls herself a 'jack of all trades, master of none' as an athlete. She played netball for Victoria but not quite for Australia, and she competed in athletics nationally but only as part of the second-string. She suffered five stress fractures in her back by the time she was 17 because she's hyper-mobile. She spent two years in rehab, which inspired her to work out the technical and physical parts of preparing for sports.

I had to be straight with her. 'I've been sitting on the couch,' I admitted. 'I haven't done anything. And I'll probably regret this – but do you want to help me give this thing another crack?'

'It'll be a grind,' she told me, 'but I'm keen to get stuck in.'

I was too, and so we began training back at Melbourne. This is that part where the movie of my life would pause and become a training montage, set to music, like something out of *The Karate Kid* ('You're the Best' by Joe Esposito) or *Rocky* ('Eye of the Tiger' by Survivor). We got on bikes and rode to parks or alongside rivers and creeks. We did boxing sessions on the beach, and afterwards ran the stairs – up and down – between the shore and the sand.

Push-ups and standing leaps. Deadlifts and medicine ball rotations. I did rope courses at Clip and Climb – one of those places where kids have birthday parties and scale obstacles with names like Astroball and Spaghetti. Narelle taught me to love training again and she began shaping my body into a weapon.

My comeback to professional tennis began in fits and starts. When I left tennis in 2014, I could have sought a 'protected ranking' – I was ranked 186 in the world at the time – but I didn't because I wanted the cleanest possible break.

Now I was back to that level of play, and I started to rise from no rank to 180 in the world in just a year. All my hard work had restored me to myself, and I was ready to go further. In 2017, my comeback was complete when I breezed past Japanese baseliner Nao Hibino, 6-3, 6-2, to win my first ever WTA title. The trophy I received was a kind of crystal vase and I gave it to someone special: my manager, Nikki Mathias.

Nikki grew up in regional Victoria, where her parents were cattle and sheep farmers. When she was eight they moved over the border to New South Wales, to a rice farm in the middle of nowhere, but she loved it. Life on the land suits some people in that way – you have family, friends and the farm. Nikki found her way in the world by leaning on those pillars. Her partner was Ben Mathias, who had coached and chaperoned me on a few junior tours. I liked her. And I knew she would be a warrior for me. I wanted to start from scratch with her. I needed her, too, and right away, as Ash Barty 2.0 was becoming a journey.

In 2017 I started taking down big names for the first time in my life. In June, I beat Garbiñe Muguruza and Barbora Strýcová, and was ranked 54. In August I beat Venus Williams and was ranked 37. In September I beat Johanna Konta, Agnieszka Radwańska, Karolína Plíšková and Jeļena Ostapenko and was ranked 23. In November I beat Anastasia Pavlyuchenkova and Angelique Kerber and finished the year ranked 17 in the world, higher than any other Australian, male or female.

So many big things were yet to come. I was ready to attack 2018, but of course I had no idea what was just around the corner.

* * *

I hear two voices when I'm playing tennis. I always have. One whispers, 'Ash, you're not good enough,' and the other replies, 'Yes, you are – come on, Ash!'

Those voices both sound true because both belong to me. One voice cuts deep into my confidence. The other lifts me up. They're so familiar, so convincing, so confusing. Both can have an impact.

So which version of myself do I listen to? That depends on timing, and circumstance, and mood. It depends on which voice calls to me more loudly. On which one *demands* to be heard. Maybe what matters most is which version of me is listening.

Today, Saturday, 7 July 2018, I'm on the No. 3 Court at the All England Lawn Tennis and Croquet Club – Wimbledon. And all I'm listening to – at least, all I can hear – is: 'Ash, you're not good enough.'

I want to cry.

Why do *I* have to be this way?

This is Wimbledon. It should be one of the joys of professional tennis to play here.

It's not for me today, with that hateful, doubting voice getting louder and louder.

Have you heard the Native American tale of the two wolves? It's a Cherokee proverb – a story about a young man who asks his grandfather about the painful struggle and fight between the two growling wolves inside of him. One wolf is evil. The other wolf is good. They are both trying to control the young man.

The young man asks: 'Which wolf will win?'

The grandfather answers: 'The one you feed.'

There's always a choice to be made between fear and faith, between 'Ash, you're not good enough' and 'Yes, you are – come on, Ash'.

Today, I feed the wrong wolf.

In truth, I've been doing this for a while, and now it spills over in the very public spotlight. What's happening? In tennis terms, I'm redlining. In other words, I'm panicking.

Wimbledon is what I watched as a little girl, and the title I dream most of winning. But for me, ambition leads to worry.

There are things I like here. I like the nice little home I'm staying in here. I like meeting the other girls on tour and the training. I like the fact that my coach, Craig Tyzzer, has forgotten to bring white shorts with him, and has to make a run to TK Maxx and Sports Direct, and all he can find there are these big, baggy white soccer shorts. Tyzz doesn't like it, but he has to pull them up, fold them over and tighten the drawstring, because he won't be allowed on the courts of Wimbledon without wearing white – and this is very, very funny to me, because the old guy looks ridiculous.

We walk through the gates of the All England Club earlier than most, and find it eerie and still. The ground staff are only just setting up, mowing and testing the soil and marking the lines. I have a hit with Jo Konta and it's heaven. I feel good about this Wimbledon.

In the first round I play Stefanie Vögele, a Swiss girl who's older than me and whom I should beat, but I have to dig in and fight.

I'm frustrated. I slam my racquet into my leg, though I know I shouldn't. I *shouldn't* let my opponent know I'm bothered. In every tiny error I see a big failure.

I come off court with a win but feel tired and annoyed. Not a good sign.

Next I play Genie Bouchard, and the media builds the match up. I get caught up in it and begin to imagine how it will be a big contest. Usually, I read nothing about myself. I listen to nothing. I turn off the television.

We play right beneath the view from the players' restaurant. I start well, but the second set I get broken out of nowhere, and the stress builds.

There are two voices inside me now. One sounds wise – 'Change your positioning, throw something unexpected her way, apply the pressure to her weaker side' – but the other is stubborn – 'Nah, I like my patterns, I'm keeping them, because I want to make this particular serve.' Somehow I scrape through and win the match.

I must face Daria Kasatkina for a place in the fourth round. That's new territory for me at this point of my career: the chance to advance to the second week of a Grand Slam.

I feel the match with Kasatkina flowing for me early. I'm quickly up 4-1, and I begin talking to myself. *I know I'm a good grass-court player*, I think. *And I know I'm a better grass-court player than her.*

Grass-court tennis is quick, with lower balls and fewer rallies. My expectations build because I'm cruising – and then something shifts.

Kasatkina begins using shape. She slows down her ball speed and controls her racquet-head speed. She hits it high and slow over the net. She puts the ball into my backhand corner, and does so again and again. She's not trying to hit winners, only to control the speed of the play.

This is designed to annoy me – and it does. She takes control of every point.

It's a small change but it throws me.

The issue is that my good is great, but my bad is horrible. When I'm winning, I look like a million bucks but when my tactics aren't working, I lack the maturity to solve my own problems. Basically, when Plan A isn't getting the job done, I can see no other options, even if plans B, C, D and E are right there in front of me.

Plan F – yelling and muttering and grumbling – seems simpler. So that's what I do.

I'm a 22-year-old highly trained professional athlete, but in this moment I decide on a public tantrum. As the points and games fall Kasatkina's way, I shake my head and grimace, and I backchat with my box – with my family and friends and supporters, and mostly with my coach.

I lose the match in straight sets: 5-7, 3-6.

Today, my childhood dream disappears. I can't look at myself in the mirror.

After, Tyzz doesn't speak to me. He leaves immediately after the match, without a word. I learn that he left the courts where I'd yelled at him and publicly rejected his help. He flies home to Australia the next day.

I can't bring myself to call him, so I send messages, texting rapid-fire apologies over and over.

His response is swift and short: *We'll talk about this at a later date. We'll work through this.* He asks a few questions, too. What was I yelling? What was I trying to say?

I call him days later, to apologise and explain.

I was trying to say that I wanted to hear from Tyzz and Tyzz only. Not to hear cheering from my manager, my boyfriend or my trainer. Not to hear 'Come on, Ash' or 'Let's go, Ash' or 'You've got this, mate'. I didn't want general support. I wanted specific direction from one voice.

Tyzz pauses before answering.

'What it looked like to us,' he tells me, 'is you telling us all to get lost.'

That breaks my heart.

Tyzz explains something carefully to me now. Something needs to change, and he's not the one who can change it. Why do I always look like I'm about to take off and then stumble? Why am I not performing as well as he knows I can?

'You are as good as every one of these girls,' Tyzz says. 'You can compete with these girls. You can *beat* these girls.' Then he's silent for a moment. 'But there is something going on in that head of yours that I have no idea how to fix. We need help.'

Attacking the Bend

I need help. I know what will happen if I try to sweep aside this Wimbledon loss – it'll happen again. And again. I need to figure this thing out.

Tyzz knows who can help. His name is Ben Crowe, a leadership expert and mindset coach – whatever that means. I learn that Ben Crowe went to university in the 1980s and later worked at Nike as their youngest ever executive. He spent decades helping athletes understand their own stories. He developed deep relationships with world champion surfers and Olympic gold medallists, Fortune 500 executives and special forces soldiers.

And that all sounds great, but I don't know this guy. Until this moment I've never heard of him. Tyzz tells me he's been thinking about bringing Crowey into the fold for a while now, but now is the time. Why? I needed to hit 'rock bottom' before he made that call.

'There is no point in you talking to someone if you're not ready to hear what they have to say,' he tells me. 'You weren't ready to accept help before. Now you are.'

He's right. I needed to know I couldn't do everything on my own, and I can see that now.

'Ash, this is how we can improve,' he says, not sure if I'm sure, 'but you've gotta be all in. You've gotta invest. You've gotta trust me.'

Of course I trust him. Tyzz is the person I trust most.

And so, I fly down to Melbourne and drive to

Crowey's office. It's winter, cold and bitter, and I'm glad to step into the warmth of his office. It's a slick space, and he seems like a cool person. He wears a thin woollen jumper with the sleeves pushed up to the elbows, and he gestures to a couch. He smiles, then he looks me in my eyes and holds my gaze. I look away, and my gaze settles on his walls.

There's a picture of Andre Agassi. A cricket shoe signed by Shane Warne. A replica of the suit worn by Cathy Freeman at the Sydney Olympics.

They say it's not what you know but who you know, and for me, who Crowey knows counts for everything. Understanding that these great sportspeople trusted him helps me offer up that same trust now. I ask him about them, trying not to pry too much, and I soon realise that Crowey has a deft way of framing their frailties as lessons.

In her documentary about the 2000 Olympics, Cathy tells how she planned her stunning gold medal race. She worked with an acronym – FLAG – that helped her break up that famous 400-metre dash into four 100-metre sections. F stood for 'Fly out of the blocks'. L was for 'Leg speed in the back straight'. A for 'Attack the bend', and G for 'Go girl, go'. Crowey tells me how she developed an entire framework for success, including a mantra, which she repeated over and over again as she walked onto the track and up to the starting line: 'Do what you know. Do what you know. Do what you know.'

This is called a 'courage mantra', Crowey tells me, and he explains that you can develop your own by asking yourself three personal questions.

The first is: 'How do I show up when I'm nervous?' Do I go to silence or violence? Fight, flight or freeze? Do my cheeks go red? Do I hope no one asks me a question? Do I name-drop? Do I argue?

All I can think in this moment is, *Do I shout at the ones I love?* and *Do I push them away at Wimbledon?*

The second question is: 'When does it happen?' Is it when I feel judged? Is it when people are staring at me? Is it when I feel like I'm losing control of a situation, or a match?

Again, all I can think of are those moments within games when nothing will go the way I want.

Finally, Crowey says, I need to ask: 'What can I say to myself the next time it happens?' What can I *think* that reminds me of strength, and not weakness?

This is the essence of the courage mantra – the words that will make you a warrior and not a worrier. The Richmond Football Club's superstar midfielder Dustin Martin repeats three words to himself in those moments when he experiences even a trace of doubt: 'Strong. Aggressive. Unstoppable.' World champion surfer Steph Gilmore says to herself, 'I love this challenge' and 'Breathe in the energy around me'.

Crowey explains to me that these kinds of sayings – from 'I'm imperfect but I'm worthy' to 'I'm enough' – can help you find a way to overcome doubts and distractions. He tells me all this – about his life and his work, about who he is and what he does – and then he smiles again, and holds my gaze once more.

Now I'm tearing up and so Crowey pushes a box of tissues towards me on the coffee table between us, rests back in his chair and gestures to me. 'Ash,' he says, 'what's your story?'

For the first time in my life, I tell someone my tale. From the time I first picked up a racquet, to packing my things away at Wimbledon less than a fortnight ago. I cry throughout. Truthfully, I weep. I *talk* and I weep. I *weep* and I talk. For four hours. Through pivotal moments and crucial relationships and a second box of tissues. I say it all out loud, and Crowey listens. It feels like an out-of-body experience. It is incredibly powerful, and absolutely terrifying.

When I finish speaking, Crowey thanks me. I feel heard, understood by this man, and I feel also as though I understand myself better too. I sip water and sigh now, and breathe deeply, emotionally exhausted.

Crowey explains that what I'm experiencing is common in elite athletes. 'Athletes have a bad habit of coming to understand their life story only through their career,' he says, 'mistaking the games we play for the people we are.' He tells me I need to forgive and change and reframe. Now that I've told my full story, he says, I need to find my *true* story.

The next morning the world seems new, but it's strange too. I meet Crowey for breakfast. I'm still tired, but we have work to do. He has important questions for me to answer – 'Who am I? What do I want? What are my values?' – but I'm stuck for a response.

He approaches me from all angles, giving me every chance to find my voice. 'What are your dreams, Ash? What are your needs? What motivates you?'

I look away and strain for something to say. I hold on to a half-thought but it slips away. I stare back at him, flustered and apologetic. I've got nothing. Later that day I fly home to Brisbane.

My manager, Nikki Mathias, calls Crowey, excited and nervous, wondering how our meetings were. He tells her the truth. 'It went incredibly well but … something is still missing. I don't know where she wants to go from here,' Crowey says. 'I don't know if she's ready. Does she actually want to do this?'

A few days later, he gets in touch with me directly. He's summarised our sessions. He's looked at my issues and tells me exactly what happened on those English grass courts at Wimbledon.

I hadn't simply stumbled on a crack in my game, he explains, but rather I was cracking up. And for it to happen in such a pronounced way – for me to turn to uncontrollable anger, to lose the plot, knowing I was hurting someone and yet not caring – was not unexpected either.

It's about self-worth, Crowey tells me. If we don't reconcile our self-worth, we tell a story of shame.

We develop imposter syndrome. Or we put up ego defences. We deny – 'I'm not really losing this' – or we rationalise – 'I'm not getting the advice I need from my team'. And once those excuses don't work, we melt down.

Rock bottom? Yep, that was me.

Crowey has talked with Tyzz, too, because my coach needs to understand what happened out there. He needs to know why I began yelling at my closest supporters.

'You understand what Ash was doing?' Crowey told him. 'She was striking out at the ones she loves, because you were the nearest and dearest thing. Think of it like being out in the ocean, and Ash is drowning. Who is she going to reach out to? Is she going to reach out quietly?'

I begin to feel something shift now, and not just because someone has helped me have an epiphany, but because Tyzz and Crowey have spoken. It feels as though we're forming a team, and reaching a common understanding. As they say, a problem shared is a problem halved.

After Crowey presents his findings to me, he asks me a question: 'Do you want to continue working?'

I grin as I speak into the phone: 'Absolutely.'

Toothaches and Toilet Breaks

I'm a sponge now. My mind craves the messages Crowey delivers, even if it's not easy to adjust to a new way of thinking. He warns me that it will be messy and confusing to reframe my mind – I will need to build it up like a muscle. *Don't be in a rush,* he writes, *and have compassion for yourself. Remember: 'I am Imperfect and Worthy'*.

This is how I feel now, in my first match after last month's Wimbledon meltdown. I play the Rogers Cup in Montreal in early August 2018 and first up

I'm facing Irina-Camelia Begu. The Romanian is five years older than me, and fiery, and not in a pleasant mood. It's been raining all morning and we've both had barely ten minutes to warm up. Late in the third set I'm down a break, and we fight over one long point. I scrap and chase and cover every inch of the playing space, and finish with a cross-court forehand pass on the run, and I know in this moment that I will win.

This little victory means nothing but stands for everything. In my next games I am sharp. In the semi-final, I think I'll be up against reigning French Open champion Simona Halep. I message Crowey, anxious and looking for help.

'Already I'm thinking about trying to figure out a way to try and compete with a world #1,' I type into WhatsApp. 'And she hasn't even won the match yet …'

'Is it strategic thinking or stressful (distracted) thinking?' Crowey asks.

'Stressful. I don't know if I can even compete with her.'

'This is a great test for you,' he replies. 'This is where acceptance and letting go come into play again. You have no control over Halep, so focusing on it is stressful. Her ranking is irrelevant. So is yours. Remember – no expectations, other than your words (calm, clear, present, sharp, etc.). That way you've got nothing to lose and everything to gain. You lighten up and just play – and the rest will take care of itself. You are a good person, Ash Barty. And a good tennis player. And you are worthy!'

I lose to Halep in the semi-final but I learn. Immediately I want to play her again. I don't want to hide away, or sulk or worry. I play her again in Cincinnati a week or so later and she beats me again. But coming off the court, all I want to do is work. I'm not seeing the defeats anymore – only the challenge. Something inside me is changing.

We go to Flushing Meadows soon after. The fans sit for hours in the heat, cooled only by icy drinks. It's sweaty and noisy and glorious – or at least that's what it looks like to me. I only get to see all that from court level.

I haven't been past the third round here, but this time I go into what is probably the biggest match of my Grand Slam career so far, against Karolína Plíšková. Typically, our matches have been close – she's always been a good test for me. Today, I lose 6-4, 6-4 and walk off the court disappointed but thinking clearly, focusing on what I did well as well as what I did poorly. *Yep, I lost that tennis match*, I think to myself, *and it's okay*.

What I'm learning and practising and experiencing for the first time is acceptance. It shines through in all the quotes Crowey and I share with one another. Some of the lines are modern, like that of American soccer icon Mia Hamm: 'Somewhere behind the athlete you've become and the hours you've practised and the coaches who have pushed you ... is the little girl who fell in love with the game and never looked back. Play for her.' Others are historical, like that of former US First Lady Eleanor Roosevelt: 'The future belongs to those who believe in the beauty of their dreams.'

The thread running through them all is that everyone is human, and imperfect, and that's okay. It's *better* than okay, actually, because it means we're all unique.

My favourite quote is known as 'The Man in the Arena'. US President Theodore Roosevelt delivered it within his 'Citizenship in a Republic' speech in Paris in 1910. It's about coming into contact with life's many and messy realities.

> *It is not the critic who counts; not the man who points out how the strong man stumbles, or where the doer of deeds could have done them better. The credit belongs to the man who is actually in*

the arena, whose face is marred by dust and sweat and blood; who strives valiantly; who errs, who comes short again and again, because there is no effort without error and shortcoming; but who does actually strive to do the deeds; who knows great enthusiasms, the great devotions; who spends himself in a worthy cause; who at the best knows in the end the triumph of high achievement, and who at the worst, if he fails, at least fails while daring greatly, so that his place shall never be with those cold and timid souls who neither know victory nor defeat.

Here's the thing. That speech is so popular with athletes, and I think that's mostly because they see themselves as the main characters and they see the critics as the writers or commentators or the many voices on social media.

But I like it because the hero has moments of failure. Look deep into the words. The strong man

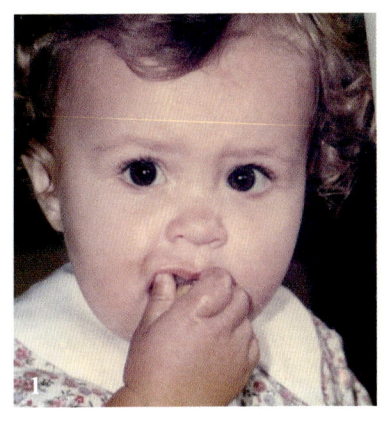

1 A very young me in 1997, eating a biscuit. Mum tells me that Digestives were my favourites.

2 On Court 3 at West Brisbane Tennis Centre, 2003, after I won one of my first trophies – the photo the entire world has seen time and time again.

3 Grade 2 school photo. I loved learning at school and met some of my best friends during my early years at Woodcrest State College. To this day, they are still some of my favourite mates and fondest memories.

4 Mum, Dad, my sisters and me on the verandah at my aunty and uncle's house in Toowoomba, where we would visit for Easter weekend. We got such a kick out of seeing the chickens they had on the property.

Growing up

Junior Wimbledon

1 With my trophy on Court 1 of the All England Lawn Tennis and Croquet Club, after defeating Irina Khromacheva in the final of the Wimbledon Girls' Singles, London, 3 July 2011. A moment that changed my life and career forever.

2 Seeing Evonne for the first time after I won Junior Wimbledon. At the Queensland Tennis Centre, Tennyson, July 2011. It was the start of an important friendship, and I will be forever grateful to Evonne for her guidance and support during my life and career.

Cricket

Batting for Brisbane Heat, my first runs in the inaugural Women's Big Bash League season, Junction Oval in Melbourne, 5 December 2015. I went on to make 39 runs off 27 balls in that innings against the Melbourne Stars.

Representing Australia

1 Casey and me celebrating our doubles win during the Fed Cup tie v Ukraine, in Canberra, 11 February 2018. It was the win that clinched the tournament 3-2 for Australia, and was also Casey's last professional match.

2 On the podium with John Peers, celebrating our bronze medal win at the 2020 Olympic Games in Tokyo – one of the proudest moments in my entire career. John and I have also played mixed doubles together at the Australian Open, Wimbledon and the US Open – there was no one else I wanted to partner with for the Olympics.

Team Work

1 My team. My family. The people who have dedicated so much time and energy to my life and career. The 2022 Australian Open final was the first time in my professional career that they were all together to see me play live.
(L–R: Nikki, Tyzz, Ali, Mum, me, Garry, Sara, Dad and Crowey)

2 Celebrating my 2022 Australian Open win with my three tennis father figures: Jim, Stolts and Tyzz. Having the three of them gather together for a beer was a special moment.

WTA Tour

1 Winning my first WTA tour event, Kuala Lumpur, 5 March 2017 – a moment to be cherished when I learned I had broken into the Top 100. An incredible week capped off by winning the doubles with Casey as well.

2 Holding the Billie Jean King Trophy after winning the WTA Finals in Shenzhen in 2019. This was one of the biggest wins of my career and I remember playing some of my best tennis during that event. An incredible week was made extra special by finishing as the WTA Year-End World No. 1 for the first time.

Doubles

Finally – a Grand Slam doubles title! Kissing the US Open women's doubles trophy with Coco Vandeweghe, New York, 10 September 2018. We saved multiple match points in the final and eventually won 3-6, 7-6 (7-2), 7-6 (8-6). Having lost five other Slam doubles finals, this was a moment to celebrate.

French Open

1 Sliding into a defensive slice backhand during my quarter-final match against Madison Keys on Court Suzanne Lenglen, Paris, 6 June 2019. It was the first time I had broken through to make a Grand Slam semi-final.

2 Taking a moment to soak in my maiden Grand Slam victory during the on-court ceremony on Court Philippe Chatrier, 8 June 2019. I played one of the best matches of my career and savoured every moment when accepting the Coupe Suzanne Lenglen.

Wimbledon

1 Playing my first-round match on Court 12 against Stefanie Vögele, Wimbledon, 3 July 2018. Having felt confident going into the 2018 Championship, it turned out to be the toughest fortnight of my career and the tournament when I hit rock bottom.

2 Box celebration. Celebrating the moment that we became the winner of the 2021 Ladies' Singles Championship. My favourite photo of my amazing, caring and loyal team.

3 My favourite photo from the journey of a lifetime. Looking at my coach, Craig Tyzzer, after winning the 2021 Wimbledon Ladies' Singles Championship, 10 July 2021. Tyzz was the person who challenged me, pushed me and drove me to be the best I could be. He was also the first to wrap his arms around me, listen to my tears and make me laugh. I will be forever in debt to him for his love, effort and professionalism.

4 Kissing the most iconic trophy in our sport: the Venus Rosewater Dish. It was such an elegant on-court ceremony – emotional and filled with tradition – that included the trophy being presented by Kate Middleton, then Duchess of Cambridge. I'll always remember the moment I took a quick glance at my team and they beamed with pride.

Australian Open

1 Celebrating becoming the Australian Open Champion, 29 January 2022. Having played some of my career-best tennis during the tournament, being presented the Daphne Akhurst Memorial Cup by Evonne Goolagong Cawley was one of my most cherished memories. It made this kiss even more special.

2 An incredible moment sharing my Australian Open victory with Cathy Freeman and Evonne just moments after I walked off court. My mentors, my mates and, most importantly, my sisters.

First Nations Community

Celebrating the 2022 Australian Open title after our Racquets and Red Dust program in the heart of our nation, Uluru. The most picturesque tennis court I've ever played on.

Family

The Future

1 Girls' weekend away. Me, Mum, Sara, Ali, Lucy and Olivia, on the Sunshine Coast. The first time all six of us had gone away together for a quiet weekend.

2 Dad, me and Mum at the Queensland Tennis Centre. I was doing a sponsor photoshoot and pulled them in for a photo.

3 Garry and me, on our wedding day in 2022.

4 The Wolfpack: Origi, Chino and Affie.

5 Reading the Little Ash books to Lucy and some of her friends. I loved reading as a kid, and I hope these books will encourage a love of reading in children.

stumbles. Despite shortcomings, he strives. He knows triumph and failure. He knows great devotion. And that's me, in my life and my career. It is what it is. I am who I am. Whatever happens, the universe is working for me, not against me. The 'Man in the Arena' quote reminds me that I can put my hopes and dreams into the world and just see what happens.

And what happens is victory, finally, in Zhuhai in November 2018. I find myself in the final there against local favourite Wang Qiang, and win the biggest tournament of my career so far – the WTA Elite Trophy. I take out the match in straight sets, and walk off court happy with the way I played, knowing that the win or loss doesn't at all change who I am.

I'm getting ready to do my press conference when Tyzz confirms this, grinning: 'You're going to finish the year as the number 15 player in the world.'

* * *

I did not imagine ringing in the New Year or the new season from a hospital bed, but here I am at Royal Perth Hospital on the afternoon of 31 December 2018. It's my wisdom teeth. I had all four removed in late November, in an attempt to eliminate problems further down the track. It turned into more of an issue. Antibiotics settled down the initial infection, but the irritation had worsened. I'm at a women's cricket match with my boyfriend, Garry Kissick, when the pain settles in and sends me to the emergency room.

I've never had a needle in my mouth before, and I'm scared. I demand that the dentist apply some numbing gel before giving me a local anaesthetic injection. Children's numbing gel. My physiotherapist is with me and is laughing loudly at my cowardice. She knows I'm a wimp.

I go to the tournament's gala ball that night with my mouth restitched and swollen. I try to eat but my lips are still numb. I give an interview on the red carpet and have to concentrate hard to avoid stumbling over my words. I pretend I'm back on tour in Europe, where I always try to take extra care when speaking, enunciating clearly and playing up my accent. 'It's so greaaat to be here. Everyone has been awwwwesome.'

It always feels as though the entire country is waiting to see what unfolds at the Australian Open. It's a stunning summer spectacle, but the hope of the nation can become a burden – or you can let it lift you up, with the lightness of excitement.

There's no point pretending the Australian Open is a tournament like any other, because it's not. It's hard to get practice courts, and impossible to get time alone. Your ever-expanding circle seems to swell from four to 40. Everyone has a question. Everyone sends a text. Everyone wants that interaction, and if you give a little piece to all of them – pausing for each conversation, stopping for every selfie, answering all those DMs – then soon you don't have anything left for yourself. The attention comes from a great place, but it can be tiring.

This year my Australian Open experience feels bizarrely calm. I train. I play. I do media. I leave. That schedule can turn into a vicious cycle, where somehow four hours have passed too quickly and the next event is you. But I feel none of that.

I have no problems in the first few rounds. Momentum is building, and I face Maria Sharapova in the fourth round.

I've never felt excitement like this before. I'm almost not myself. Maria is a champion. A figure in the firmament. She's an aggressive, first-strike player and loves getting in your face. Back in 2012, in Brisbane, an injury robbed me of the opportunity to play her. I want this match-up – badly.

In the first set, I'm feeling like I have to play the best match of my career to win. I press too much, and lose my way. In the second set I have to fight and adjust. I read her patterns better, sit on her serve and change the dynamic, and I win the second set. I offer a big fist-pump to my team: *I'm not going anywhere!* The noise and energy in Rod Laver Arena is extraordinary. I am so ready.

Now Maria takes a bathroom break. I think I've taken all of two bathroom breaks in my life. I'd love to know how many players genuinely go to the toilet, and how many are simply using the break to stop negative momentum and recover. It's within the rules, but often it's questionable.

After the seventh minute, this break from Sharapova begins to feel tactical – and the crowd don't like it. I have to tell myself not to look over at my box, because if I make eye contact with Tyzz I'll laugh, and that laugh will be picked up on camera, and then people will think I'm smirking while the home crowd jeers. Finally, Maria walks back onto the court and I can't help but grin, and that syncs up with the booing of the crowd. But I don't care anymore.

When I want to stay in the moment on court, I often use a little breathing exercise: close eyes, inhale, smile. But I have other ways. Right now I see the Spidercam zooming above me on its cables. Sometimes I try to hit it during warm-up, and now I chuck a ball at it for the same giggle. As Crowey likes to say, 'Lighten up or tighten up.'

Against the strength of the towering Russian five-time Grand Slam champion, I play brilliant tennis. I lighten up and hit aces. She tightens up and hits double faults. After two hours and 22 minutes I win. I'm through to the quarter-finals – the first Australian woman in ten years. I am 22 years old, and this is the most satisfying victory of my career so far.

There's no fairy tale for me in the next game, though, against Petra. On a cool evening, she coolly hits everything out of the middle, and I can't find myself. She crushes me. Simply put, Petra has my measure – but whenever you walk to the net after playing her, you instantly forget who's won and who's lost because there's always a smile.

I wave goodbye to the crowd and do my interviews. I sleep and fly home to Brisbane. I unpack and reset. Every tournament ends this way – like some sort of fly-in, fly-out stealth mission – but the Australian Open is always such a whirlwind. You lose and leave, and love the experience anyway.

Besides, I'm not dwelling on the loss. I'm thinking about how our limited and interrupted preparation didn't unsettle me. I'm thinking about toothaches and hot winds. I'm thinking about finally beating Simo. I'm thinking about knocking over Maria Sharapova in an epic, and I'm thinking about what Crowey said to me in the gym after my game with Maria: 'That's one of the strongest displays of performance mindset that I've seen.'

I'm a different player now, I think to myself. *I'm a different person.*

Bullrings and Baguettes

Jessica Pegula. I don't recognise the name. She's American, apparently. I've never seen this girl hit a ball, which makes it a tricky way to begin my 2019 French Open.

Usually, a bit of unfamiliarity doesn't matter too much but I still like to understand how my opponent swings their racquet. People think elite athletes have perfect vision and freakish reaction time – and often they do – but so much of that relies on understanding of the game. Often, you're not *seeing* the ball better but instead *reading* it better. All through repetition.

Pegula and I play on Court 1, which is also known as the Bullring. It's a 1970s concrete structure with 3800 seats and thunderous acoustics.

My encounter with Jess is scratchy – normal for the first match in a Grand Slam tournament, really. If you're seeing the ball like a watermelon and crushing everything in sight at this stage, it's almost not right. In a way, a challenge is what you want first: to experience a few nerves but then settle them enough to win. In this case 6-3, 6-3. I'm settled now, and ready to build.

Roland-Garros holds a strange importance for me. I was never the type of kid to sit in front of the TV watching tennis at 2 am, but I did once, in 2010. Sam Stosur was in the final, and I dragged my mattress out into the living room to watch every point. That was special.

A year later, I was there in person as a junior. I won in the first round – my first victory at a junior Grand Slam.

They say the crowds at Roland-Garros are more discerning than most, and you feel that, too. They're more aware of the crucial shifting moments and the subtlety of great shots.

On this day, against Danielle Collins, I want to stamp my authority and make a statement – which is difficult when the 63 other girls left in the draw are trying to do the same thing. Collins fights me in the first set, an arm wrestle that I win 7-5, but I'm able to put my foot down and create more pressure in the second set, which I win 6-1.

By the fourth round, I'm ready to feel anxious, and so I turn to those closest to me. In truth, I lean on them. If not now, then when? I know Garry is coming over soon, as are Jim, Dad and Mum. I FaceTime with my sisters and my niece Lucy and nephew Oscar. I feel as relaxed as possible coming into my match against Sofia Kenin, who makes me uncomfortable. Her unpredictable patterns often take away my rhythm.

It's overcast and drizzling, and conditions are heavy. I hit almost a dozen unreturnable serves and aces to start the match. But I lose myself tactically, temporarily forgetting that I can't keep the ball away from her racquet all day. Maybe that's why we suddenly find ourselves with one set each: 6-3, 3-6.

That's when I take a moment to think. *Regardless of whether I win or lose this match it'll be a statement about how I approach the game and how I want to play.*

I streamroll her in the final set, 6-0, and walk off court ready to play in my first Grand Slam quarter-final with Madison Keys. Only two years ago at this event, she knocked me over in 55 minutes, using her power to bully and embarrass me right off the court.

I have to take her kick serve and first strike away from her. Her kick serve is a weapon, and when you take away a weapon you make a player feel as though they're competing with one arm tied behind their back. In the case of her hopper, I'll stand back and wait for the high bounce, and on every second serve I know I have to be clear in my decision-making. A big backhand middle to put her under time pressure, or a short backhand slice to bring her forward and low, into a position on the court that she doesn't like.

In the semi-final I'm playing Amanda Anisimova. She's 17, new to the tour and already making a splash, knocking over top ten players and winning events. There are worries in my head now – *So much to lose, and no excuses* – but I start on fire. I sit down at the changeover well in front, 5-0, but I'm thinking, *This isn't quite right – I've done nothing to get here.* Famous last thoughts?

My moment is over, and she breaks me, and I panic. *What have I done?*

Amanda wins one game. Then another. Then another. Then another. And another. And another.

And then she wins that first set in a tie-break, and I'm stifling tears, looking to Tyzz for something, anything. He holds his posture tall, and lifts his hands. *Chest up, mate, chest up.* But the second set continues in this way. I quickly go down a double break, 0-3. I want to stand up and be proud of my game, proud of my team, but I'm drowning – quickly. And then it starts to rain …

Amanda's team tells her to get off the court, and she argues this point with the chair umpire, who for now is saying the match will continue. I almost want to walk over and shake some sense into her. *What are you doing?* I think. *Are you not seeing me?* I'm breaking before her eyes. I've won just one of the past 11 games. Now, I have been gifted a moment to reset. To think. To make a change.

I realise I have a chance. Now I rediscover that single truth about tennis, which is not true of any other sport: until you lose that final match point, you can always win.

I make up my mind: *I'm going to play the Australian way, and fight to the end. That's what Aussies do. That's what Ash Barty does.*

I want to be cool and calm but I'm feeling this game now. I'm not detached from it in some professional sense. I'm in it, and my heart is pounding.

I surge and create and find a way to win a game, and again, and again, and again, and again, and again, and the second set (6-3) is mine. I can't be stopped now, and almost before I can draw breath I've won the third set 6-3 and I'm standing at the net, leaning on the net, ready to collapse.

I feel as though I need to apologise to Amanda, and my team, even myself, for making everything feel so emotional. But the athlete and the competitor inside thinks only one thing: *If I can win a tennis match like that, I can win any tennis match.*

Tyzz sees me crying now, and slaps me on the leg. 'Mate, you're in a Grand Slam final tomorrow. No one can take that away from you.'

I speak to no one but Tyzz that night. He has encouraging things to say, but my confidence has fallen. *I don't deserve this,* I think, *I'm not worthy of being here, I'm not good enough. I'm into the final of a Slam without beating a top ten player.*

He shakes his head. 'It doesn't matter, because you've outlasted them,' he says. 'You can only beat whoever's on the other side of the net.'

I sleep for 14 hours.

I wake up on the morning of the final and pull open the curtains. It looks like Miami out there, sapphire sky and the barest puff of cloud. And it's windy – I like the wind. I pick up my phone and there's a voicemail from Casey Dellacqua, and a photo of Lucy and Oscar in their *Toy Story* pyjamas. I'm a blubbering mess and call Crowey, who calms me down.

I have the same breakfast every day – two fried eggs on a half-baguette, with a few berries on the side. I head to the courts for a half-hour warm-up, and then to pass time we play cricket. My opponent for the day – Markéta Vondroušová, a 19-year-old left-hander from Prague – sees us, and she smiles. She finds her own quiet corner to prepare.

We're called to start the match and I grab my bag. I've promised myself I'll walk onto the court smiling, no matter how I feel. I'm escorted by a beautiful young girl, who speaks only a little English, and I hold her hand and tell her, 'Hey, we have to smile, both of us, but how good is this?'

Tactics seem more important than ever now, so what do you do against someone like Markéta? She hits a mean drop shot, and my counter-plan is simple: take that weapon away from her. Be disciplined – push the ball down the line and steal the net position.

I'm in the zone quickly, and I recognise this as what Crowey calls my A game.

Before I know it, I'm pushing Markéta deep into a corner, and she flicks a lob skyward. I approach it on the bounce – the ball goes in and the match is all over: *Six-un! Six-trois!*

I don't know what to do – how should I celebrate? I don't think it through. I put my arms up, turn to my team.

Markéta is beautiful at the net. We shake the umpire's hand and everything goes numb – my legs, my shoulders. I can't hold my arms up. I crouch on the court. I thank the crowd but my greatest thanks is that this two weeks is now over.

I'm handed the Coupe Suzanne Lenglen – and I lift it up and kiss it, because it's a Grand Slam trophy. Then the national anthem is playing and my knees begin to buckle.

When it is all over, on the side of the court, my shoes scratching at the clay underfoot, I'm sitting in my chair, waving Tyzz down from the stands, and it takes him an eternity but he finally gets there. Someone takes a photo of us in that moment, hugging, but they don't know what we're saying to one another.

'No one can take this away from us,' I tell him.

'No one can take this away from *you*,' he replies.

And then I say one final thing, which prompts a look from Tyzz. It's a joke … but it's not a joke.

'Mate,' I say, 'can I retire now?'

Mortgages and Monkey Bars

It's late 2019. I'm the French Open champion and later that year, I play the Birmingham Classic – a beautiful and quiet tournament. Not so much to win as to freshen up and sharpen up. My draw is brutal, yet I feel great. I don't know how, but I'm refreshed.

I move through the draw with a mantra – *There will be noise, I will be sore, but the process will work* – and it holds me in a good place. The week becomes a study in balance. We step onto the court, and we work. We step off the court, and we relax. We do it against Venus Williams (6-4, 6-3) and then against Barbora Strýcová (6-4, 6-4), and this means something. All week I've known that if I win this tournament, I will be ranked as the number 1 player in the world, and now all I have to do is beat my current doubles partner, Julia Görges.

Winning back-to-back tournaments is rare – I've never done it before – but we are back on grass, the number 1 ranking is on the line, and my loved ones are here enjoying it with me. Game on.

I love Jules. That's not true of all my opponents. There are girls I dislike playing, and girls I just plain dislike – mostly those who can't separate who they are on and off the court. You're about to play them and they won't look you in the eye or say hello. Or you beat them and they don't talk to you for a week. Some fall into a fury when you give them a lesson during practice, unable even to train with detachment. I want to wipe the floor with those girls.

I keep track of them, too, in a little black book inside my mind. Jules is definitely not one of those girls.

I stay in the moment against her, playing each point and each ball on its merits, and the final score is 6-3, 7-5 in my favour.

I put a hand up to my mouth and over my face, because I'm laughing at the sheer absurdity of this moment. WTA World No. 1! I'm 23 years old, and the first Australian woman to top the singles rankings in 43 years. 'Wow,' I murmur to myself. 'This is real.'

* * *

Although I become World #1, I don't reach the quarter-finals at Wimbledon, and I struggle in the American hardcourt summer too. This is no cause for panic, but a conversation is required.

I fly home and ease back into myself the way I always do, waking in my own bed, walking my dogs and making my own coffee. That's a ritual for me.

I love taking my time making my coffee – searching for strong latte perfection.

But today I drink a cup made by the barista at Cheeky Monkey café in Melbourne. I'm sitting opposite Tyzz and Crowey, having the chat this moment demands – this moment where I'm doubting myself again.

I question my success. I put an asterisk next to every accomplishment. The media tells me: *You're winning, but you haven't had to beat Simona Halep or Karolína Plíšková. You're looking good but you haven't had to knock over Naomi Osaka or Serena Williams.*

They're right, I begin to think. *I haven't played anyone in the top 20.*

Crowey takes the emotion out of the moment and turns straight to logic. That's the way the system works, he tells me, it gives an advantage to the higher-ranked players so they can plough through to tougher opposition in the finals. So I'm bound to come up against lower-ranked players.

Tyzz says it doesn't even matter. Not even a little bit. What matters isn't how I play in the big moments against the top players, but how I play against everyone at every tournament.

Now I'm feeling embarrassed, as if I'm back at the West Brisbane Tennis Centre being reprimanded by Jim, and reminded that I'm not better than anyone else, even if I can hit the single slice backhand and twirl my racquet on my finger like a gunslinger.

Basically, the message Tyzz and Crowey give me is that it's okay to lose to the 47th-ranked player because, hey, they're the 47th-best tennis player in the entire damn world! They have talent and drive, and they're not here to roll over for me.

I head to Asia with this in mind, and find myself trading blows with the very best. I do well in Wuhan and lose in the semi-finals to Aryna Sabalenka (ranked 9). I continue that form in Beijing and lose in the final to Naomi Osaka (ranked 3). I move on to Shenzhen to play in the novel WTA Finals series, a contest searching for the best of the best players of 2019.

A quirk that not many people might know is that each tournament uses different tennis balls. They might look the same but they do not feel that way.

Wimbledon uses Slazenger balls, and has done since 1902, in the longest partnership in sports equipment history. Over the two-week tournament, some 54,000 balls are used there. The Australian Open uses Dunlop balls. The French Open and the US Open both use Wilson balls, although the French clay-court ball is very different from the American hardcourt ball. The US Open ball is as light as paper.

I'm in big-game mode at Shenzhen, as I'm through to the final against Elina Svitolina. She's beaten me the past five times we've played. She's a fighter who always moves well and always competes. She doesn't have a game with big weapons, but she really owns the game she has. Basically, she doesn't miss. Ever. Her strategy is simple: make balls. The more balls she hits, the more opportunities she gives me to miss, and then it becomes a game of patience. Do I wait her out? Do I take a risk?

The Shenzhen court is purple, which is strange but I enjoy it all the same. It's dark in this stadium. The lights are lowered but the playing surface is bright and there's a gigantic screen dominating one end of the arena.

Elina is the reigning champion, and this court suits her.

My body is sore today but my backhand is fluent and strong. My serve is assertive and creative. It takes time to find her breaking point, and when I do it's a mature and clinical win – 6-4, 6-3.

I celebrate with my team and give Tyzz a hug, and say to him with a smile, 'No one beats Ash Barty six times in a row.' The WTA Finals is arguably the most significant title outside of the Grand Slams. I am pretty damn proud of my week and the way

I finished the season as the WTA Year-End World No. 1.

The winner's cheque – A$6.4 million – is more prize money than has been awarded to any player at any tournament ever, male or female.

I'm a homebody who has never seen herself living anywhere but Australia and right now, I'm thinking of a new home. My forever dream home and – I hope – family home. And it's freeing to know that I can afford to buy exactly what I want. I know what I want, too. I want two storeys and a big stone fireplace and a butler's pantry. I want a floor and a bed. I settle on building a new place high on a hill near Mum and Dad.

Money has never been my motivation for playing, of course. I play for the love of the game, for the thrill of the fight, for the reward of a challenge met, and for the people who support me.

My parents had every right to resent my tennis obsession, as it changed years of family plans, but they were only ever encouraging. My sisters had every right to be jealous of the way all attention was diverted to my hobby, but they were the first ones to bake me a #1 cake. Now I want to repay them all.

Ali is a primary school teacher, taking classes for preps and Grade 1s at a small independent First Nations school. Sara is a nurse and midwife and lactation consultant at a private hospital in Ipswich. Mum and Dad both have good jobs too, but the home they raised me in isn't yet fully their own.

I don't know how long it will take for any of them to pay off their mortgages, so I do it for them.

'It's too much,' they say. 'You can't!'

But isn't this the point of money? To make life easier and more comfortable for those you love, so that they can live out their dreams? It is the best money I've ever spent. Well, that and the monkey bar set I buy for the kids for Christmas – and which I give to them a month early, because I'm soft as butter.

Spit the Dummy

After my WTA final win, I fly immediately from Shenzhen to Australia, although not for the long rest I need. You might think a Grand Slam victory plus the number 1 ranking in the world would be enough for me in 2019, but I have the Fed Cup (later known as the Billie Jean King Cup). It's a chance for women to play tennis as a team, nation against nation. Australia last won it in 1974; since then we've been runners-up a heartbreaking eight times. Now we've made it into the final for the first time in 26 years. And we're playing on our home court in Perth.

The setting in Western Australia is perfection, too: ticket sales are going wild, with a capacity crowd of 13,109 expected for both days of the two-day event at RAC Arena, not far from Kings Park and the Swan River – a record for a Fed Cup contest in this country. But all their cheering and goodwill and support can't do it for us. Our captain, Alicia Molik, makes that clear. Mol is not stern but she sure is serious. I love the way she goes about it. I love her, really.

She first learned who I was when I was only 11 – playing in the national clay-court juniors at the Glen Iris Valley Tennis Club in Melbourne. She was in her mid-20s, playing professionally and living in a share house in South Yarra. I had no idea she was there, and barely remember the game, but Mol tells me she saw a short girl using every tool in the kit – topspin, slice, drop shots, lobs – in the space of a few minutes.

We didn't actually meet until I was 15, and even then it was only quick. Mol had been watching me practise before Junior Wimbledon, just standing at the side of the court, one Aussie observing another. She saw the same skill set she had seen before, only by then it was more developed. She said hello to me, and looked me in the eye. I smiled and immediately looked down at my shuffling feet. I had manners but also nerves.

Mol is from Adelaide, and grew up playing tennis in Henley Beach for a tiny centre called Seaside Tennis Club. She never chased the idea of a professional career, but she got better quickly and was picked in state teams, and by 18 found herself representing Australia. Her first WTA title came in Tasmania at age 22. In 2004 she proudly won a bronze medal at the Athens Olympics, and stood on the dais alongside absolute giants in Amélie Mauresmo and Justine Henin. She had surprised herself when she entered the top 100. She surprised herself even more when she made the top 50. Entering the top 25 was a shock. But she truly surpassed her own expectations in 2005 when she was ranked eighth in the world.

In Perth, in our Fed Cup final against France, she is a rock.

The morning I open the play, I know I have one more big effort in me, one more day for my season. But the match drags on and I'm grimacing at every change of ends. Everything is catching up with me.

'I've got concrete in my legs,' I tell Mol. 'They're so heavy.'

'I know, mate. I know your legs are heavy. I know you feel horrible,' Mol says. 'But you've got this.'

I want to stand up in this moment and be a leader. I want to win this title for our nation. For my teammates and for Mol. I know I can, too.

But it isn't happening for me now. All the encouragement and all the self-talk and all the demands I place on myself aren't changing a thing.

I try firing up, breaking back in the third set and doing a running fist-pump and screaming into the sky. The match is a two-and-a-half-hour epic – 2-6, 6-4, 7-6 (1) – but I'm the loser.

I walk into the gym, broken, and slump on the treadmill in tears. Mol has crouched down on the treadmill next to me and I look at her through red eyes. 'I'm sorry! I'm sorry! *I'm so sorry!*' I offer up. 'If I could give back the French Open to win that match, I would.'

Mol bursts into tears now too, and gives me a hug. She wanted this just as badly as I did. It's only then that we realise Ajla Tomljanović, our teammate who is making her debut, is warming up for her singles challenge. I needed to let it all out, but not in that setting – not in a way that might affect someone else and their preparation. Athletes are strange beasts ... who knows what might make their mindset unsteady?

Oh no, I think. *What have I done?*

But Ajla walks back into the rooms 92 minutes later with a victory, and she walks straight over to me.

'I knew you always wanted this,' she says, 'but I didn't realise you wanted it that much.'

Seeing me so distraught wasn't a hindrance, she tells me; actually, it fired her up and sent her chasing the win.

We go to doubles now, a deciding rubber, with me and Sam Stosur facing Garcia and Mladenovic, and I don't know exactly what happens or why, but we don't quite gel on court. And we don't use our voices enough. We get a few unlucky points against us, and no lucky ones back. We find no momentum. Nothing clicks. And it begins to feel as though it wasn't meant to be.

We chase and lunge and try, but the French girls cruise to a 6-4, 6-3 win in the match – and a 3-2 victory in the Fed Cup. The crown is lost again.

We celebrate and mourn together at the Westin Hotel afterwards. And all our families and friends are there. Mum and Dad. Sara is there too, with my niece Lucy. And then we fly home to Brisbane, where Ali is waiting because she's about to give birth.

Now, at the end of an enormous year, I spend six hours going through all of my suitcases – washing and ironing and folding – because that's what I do when I get home.

That night, Ali gives birth to baby Olivia, and I go to the hospital the next morning and give my new niece a cuddle. When I look at the first photo I take with Liv, I cannot believe how tired I appear. I'm a shell of myself, stretched and pale and desiccated. But I'm also about to get stronger, hearty and hale, because I'm around the people I love and cocooned in the place I love. I'm finally home.

* * *

I'm crisscrossing the continent now. I fly east once more, 4000 kilometres this time, heading to the

Miami Open. I like it here. I never have time to explore, but the heat and humidity remind me of home. The Miami Dolphins stadium brings a fresh new court, a bright aqua and blue. When you get into the zone on a hot day, playing a tennis match can feel like swimming in soupy tropical waters, as you sprint and sweat and swot. It's challenging, and I like a challenge.

I've injured my foot not too long ago and I can't push off on my serve. If I chase down a point and slam on the brakes, it feels like a long needle is being pushed into my foot. I test myself with my trainer, Mark Taylor, and he holds me back a little, worried I might end up in hospital on his watch. We've worked together for a couple of years now, and he gets a bit nervous about these things.

I call him 'Tubs' because that's the nickname of his namesake, the former Australian cricket captain. Tubs hates this. He prefers his old nickname – 'Beef' – which was given to him when he worked in

British tennis, for the LTA. But he doesn't work there anymore. He began working for Tennis Australia in 2017, then he started travelling with me in 2018, so he'll just have to deal with my naming conventions. I let him be in charge in other ways.

Tubs runs my strength sessions, from warm-up to activation, from squatting to hopping to bounding, from box jumps to Romanian deadlifts. He makes me do interval sprint work – 30 seconds flat out, 30 seconds rest – and increases my maximum speed enormously. He knows I don't like running, especially on the treadmill, and puts me on the watt bike instead, because I love riding with resistance. He talks constantly about training for injury prevention, but also power. Get strong, very strong. Tubs has been building up both in me for a while.

We met at the Queensland Tennis Centre, where the Brisbane International is held. He had only been in the country a few weeks. I learned his story and liked his story. He comes from Bury St Edmunds, a small town in Suffolk, and participated in many sports as a kid – tennis, soccer, rowing, rugby. He had the desire to turn professional in all of them but never quite got there. Sport was still his biggest passion and working in physical training was the next best thing. He moved down under when he was 31, with his girlfriend, Fiona, who is now his fiancée. The weather was a shock to the system, in a pleasing way. And the change of pace – after a decade in London – was just right too. He needed to be calmed down.

Tubs can be highly strung – notoriously so, in fact. I joke with him over this, actually. It was only a few months ago that I wandered down an aisle in Woolies and a pack of pink dummies caught my eye. I thought of how Tubs is so quick to anger – how he 'spits the dummy' over the slightest things – and I came up with a game. Well, maybe it's more a rule: if anyone in our group gets too worked up, they have to wear the dummy, by attaching it to the lanyard holding their tournament accreditation.

If you get aggressive? You wear the dummy. It happens often, too.

Here's an example of how it works. We've just arrived here in Miami, and we're checking in to the Marriott. Tyzz's room isn't ready, and he's already tired and cranky, and he loses his temper at hotel reception. The rest of us have an impromptu vote: 'Dummy spit? Show of hands.' And it's settled.

Tyzz has actually had a meltdown twice here in Florida, which is uncommon for him. The other time, we were meant to be heading back to the hotel after a day of play, and the girl handling ground transport told him he'd have to wait 45 minutes until the next shuttle bus. He lost it – and he got the dummy again. Overnight this time – it's a privilege.

But Tubs is different. He wears the pink dummy 90 per cent of the time, because he's so easily wound up. Sometimes he gets annoyed answering questions from strangers about the thing around his neck, and those little tantrums mean he has to wear it even longer. He suspects a conspiracy – because there is one. He might wander away from the steel travel coffee mug he takes everywhere with him, and we hide it. That's when Tubs grouches and grumbles. Hook, line and sinker – he gets the dummy.

We're in the gym one day doing advanced hamstring stretches – a high-level deceleration exercise – and I fake a torn hammy. After the session, I pretend I'm in excruciating pain all the way into the physio's room, and I bring them in on the joke too, asking for fake strapping and treatment. They're all in. Tubs is mortified that he's broken me in the middle of a season. ('You had one job, mate ...') And then I come clean. He raises his voice and gets mad – and fair enough. But it's still a dummy spit. Maybe I went too far with this one, but it was still a bit of fun. Definitely worth it.

We work on our exercises together now in Miami, and I feel strong in his care. In my first match I destroy Dayana Yastremska, a Ukrainian teenager.

I tape up my foot and feel no pain either against Sam Stosur. I don't enjoy beating her 6-0, 6-3, but at the net she shakes my hand, and shakes her head with a rueful grin – 'Mate, that was unbelievable' – and instantly makes me feel better. Kiki Bertens is next, and the match is physical and high quality – a genuine tug of war. One of the best we've played.

Tyzz has warned me that this is where my career is now headed: I'll be in more important matches against top ten players that are not going to be one-sided. 'They're always close,' he says, 'and very little determines the outcome.' I have to accept that Kiki will produce brilliant play, and Kiki has to accept my talents, too. I win 4-6, 6-3, 6-2, and find myself facing Petra again.

It's been raining all day, and our match becomes a tussle all night. I win through tactics and composure, and I look to Tyzz and point a finger at my temple: *I thought my way through this one. We're bloody tough.*

I meet Petra at the net, and she knows what the

result means. 'Well done, Ash,' she tells me. 'There's no one more deserving of being in the top ten.'

It's the first time I've been in that group. I'm now ranked number 9. It's what I've always wanted.

I work my way calmly through aggressive Estonian baseliner Anett Kontaveit in the semi-final, and days later wake up ready for the final. I text Crowey: *It's a beautiful day*. And he replies: *What does that mean?* And it means nothing, other than that I feel calm and happy. Ready.

I'm playing Karolína Plíšková. The Czech is tall and rangy, and most would say better than me. She's a serve and first-strike specialist who only a year earlier was ranked number 1 in the world. She crushes the ball. Flat, hard, through the court. But I have a plan. I'm going to get on my bike, ride all day and use the hot southern Florida sun against her. I'll be happy if I keep her out there all afternoon.

I win the first set in a tie-breaker, going ahead at 2-1 with a 14-stroke rally. Then I wear her down physically in the second set, making sure to deny her any easy points on serve. She breaks back only once.

I'm in complete control all day, and before I know it I'm holding a tall glass trophy and orange gold streamers are raining down upon me. I've won my fourth trophy, and the biggest of my career so far. It's what's known as a Premier Mandatory title – one of the top tour events. I sign autographs on photos and racquets and big novelty tennis balls. I talk to the media and then shower and rest, and finally I pose for photos in front of the fountains outside the Hard Rock Stadium.

I write down goals at the start of every year. Asking myself, *What do I want to achieve this year?* Now I think back to my list.

I want to beat Simona. *Done.*

I want to beat Petra. *Done.*

I want to be top ten in the world. *Done.*

There's so much more to do.

Zoom Zoom

Everyone needs a steak place, and mine is Moo Moo in Brisbane. In early 2021, two days before I'm due to fly overseas on tour, I visit there with Crowey. I order a medium-rare eye fillet with mushroom sauce, and he has his usual Scotch fillet, medium. We split a side of brussels sprouts, a pear and rocket salad and a bowl of fries.

The poor waiters have to ask for our order three times, however, because I'm caught up in talking and venting.

I'm worried, I tell him, because I'm leaving the country on tour this weekend, and I know there'll be no coming home this year. Coming back to tennis, I had promised myself that I'd fly home the moment I felt I needed rest, but this isn't possible in a pandemic.

'I'm scared,' I tell Crowey. 'I don't know what this year is going to look like. I can't picture it.'

I've only ever travelled for three months at a time, and at the end of that kind of stretch I'm always fatigued and fed up.

I do know that I'm not alone in my discomfort. Other tennis players from all over the globe will be facing the same apprehension. Handling the situation better than them – if I can do that – will be an obvious advantage.

'You need to think of this year as one big adventure,' says Crowey. 'It doesn't mean it'll be easy, but you never know what might come out of it. Focus on discovering.'

We work a little on establishing my values and keep coming back to grit, and courage.

It doesn't make this thing I'm about to do any easier, though. I haven't travelled in virtually a year, and I'm about to head off on the road with no end date in sight.

I know my itinerary backwards. My bags are packed and checked, top to bottom. My travel app says the plane from Sydney to Los Angeles is delayed 12 hours, but I haven't received any alerts. That night in Brisbane becomes a flurry of phone calls between me and Tyzz and my travel agent. The booking system shows no delays. Qantas says no delays. But American Airlines says differently – their plane hasn't left the United States yet. Can Qantas reissue our connecting legs to Sydney? *Yes.* What happens if the flight to LA is delayed? *Hold, please.*

I get on the plane south, and in the domestic terminal at Sydney Airport I'm told that, because of Covid, there's no transfer bus to the international terminal anymore. I'll have to pick up my bags, get in a cab, go to international departures and check in for my flights – all in just 90 minutes. It's a nightmare. *This is the world telling me to stay in Australia*, I think. *This is everything telling me: you are doing the wrong thing, you shouldn't be doing this.* Next I am told that one of my bags is lost: my tennis bag, containing my racquets, my string, my shoes, everything. I'm barely keeping it together when the bag is finally found.

I have a few minutes in this eerily abandoned terminal, and I decide I need a notebook, so I can write down all the stuff I need to know each week in each location. It's how I keep on top of my world. *What's the hotel address? Where is the laundry? Where do I get breakfast? What day do I need to do Covid testing? Who are the physios on this swing? How do I get in and out of this arena?* I need to write it all down.

On the first page I write 'Our COVID Cootie Adventure'. I have to take the seriousness out of it, so I make it into a game of dodging playground germs. I decide to count the days, marking them in sets of five, as if I'm in prison and counting down my sentence by scratching lines on the cell wall. (I don't know it yet, but I'll end up marking 203 straight days away from home, along with 74 Covid tests.)

We land in Los Angeles and go through customs, and I learn that the private plane we booked to take us from LA to Miami is gone. We wanted to mitigate the Covid risk by flying with fewer people, but because of our 24-hour delay there are no planes available anymore. It's spring break in America, and wealthy teens have booked all the jets.

There are no seats on commercial airlines either, and if we don't leave soon we won't make the tournament cutoff. My manager, Nikki, contacts actor Chris Hemsworth's travel agent, who puts us in touch with a private jet company, but there's also a chance we can use country singer Keith Urban's personal plane. Welcome to the greatest diva moment of my life, where my ability to play tennis rests on the good graces of a Grammy Award winner and Thor. Unfortunately, the jet company we're put in touch with by the God of Thunder is already fully booked, and the private plane of the singing *American Idol* host is being serviced. Someone has two tickets on a domestic flight, and we take them in an instant, and squish like sardines into economy.

We get tested upon arrival in Florida, get to our hotel room, and you might think relief would wash over me – but instead I break down completely, knowing that this is what the year ahead might look like. *I cannot do this*, I think. *This is not what I signed up for.*

But I have to snap out of it and look for some positives. I have to dig deep for the grit and courage I know are there, because I'm desperate to defend the biggest WTA title of my career to date. *Whoever does it best will win*, I remember. *This is the year of adventure*, I think.

* * *

There has been a lot of chatter about who deserves to be the WTA World No. 1. I don't follow it much, but I know a lot of people think I'm undeserving of the rank, particularly after Naomi Osaka wins the 2020 US Open and the 2021 Australian Open, two Slams in succession. This gets to me a little bit, and fires me up.

Don't listen to the haters, I think. *I am world number 1, and I know I'm the best tennis player in the world at the moment.*

I go into the final of the Miami Open. To all those who don't believe in me, I send a silent message: *Stop talking and watch me play.*

I'm up against Bianca Andreescu, whom I've never played before, but I know her matches aren't stress-free. A lot of them are close and there's always drama. She creates and craves the drama, thrives on it, but she turns up for the big points. The conditions are brutal, with cold, gusting winds. At first I can't hit the side of a truck, but I adjust and she can't find the court. Whoever handles it better, right? It's an odd, muted finish, because I'm up a set and two breaks – 6-3, 4-0 – when she retires hurt.

I go into the press conference, and still want to unload on anyone talking me down. *Whether you think I deserve to be here or not, I know I deserve to be here – end of story*, I am thinking. But I don't need to say anything to them. I've retained the number 1 ranking. I have nothing I need to prove by making public comments like that. My tennis does it for me.

* * *

The tournament in Stuttgart has always been voted the best WTA 500 tournament, yet I've never been, despite the significant carrot they dangle. The city is described as 'the cradle of the automobile' – the home of Mercedes-Benz and Porsche – so the tournament offers a unique prize. If you're a top five player in the world and you win a single round, you get a free Porsche. Win the entire thing, you get another free Porsche. I want to win a Porsche. Or two.

The contests are played on an indoor synthetic clay – the only surface I haven't yet won on – and I make my way through the early rounds. That might sound as though I'm cruising through opposition with ease, like steel splitting wood, but each match takes grit and resilience, coping skills and consideration.

In the final, against Aryna Sabalenka, she's seeing the ball like a watermelon, and I lose the first set 3-6. In truth, I'm lucky it's that close.

'Tyzz,' I say. 'I'm not even in this. I'm getting rag-dolled here.' He tells me to find a way, and for me it becomes pressure on her serve, and pressure through my serve – getting on top of her at the start of every point, until she loses her head. The battle is mine.

And so, in the week of my 25th birthday, I end up winning two Porsches, which is completely mad – especially as I already have a Porsche at home, awarded to me in 2019 for finishing the year as the world number 1. I barely ever drive it.

Still, the experience is fun, and all part of that spirit of adventure – the hero's journey of discovery. Before I move on to the next challenge of 2021, after match point in this German city, I turn to Tyzz with a cheeky smile and a few choice words: 'Zoom zoom.'

25 Per Cent Effort

The 2021 French Open is coming. But I can't handle Paris too early, which is why we have flown to the south of France, to a place called Beaulieu-sur-Mer, just outside of Nice.

In little hamlets like this, the French Riviera is quaint but stunning, like a European dream.

We've come here because it's quiet, but this is the week of the Formula 1 Grand Prix in nearby Monaco, so a parade of Ferraris and McLarens and Aston Martins prowl past.

It sounds glamorous but we keep things sensible. We are here to enjoy but we are here to work.

We train in the morning on one of five courts in a tiny tennis club that almost feels like someone's opulent backyard. I hit plenty of balls and physically I feel great. The days are long in the best way. We have time on our side, and no need to rush – the perfect preparation for Roland-Garros. I have never felt more prepared for a Grand Slam.

All good things must end, and we head northwest to Paris. I'm back in the City of Love and staying in a nice hotel, but I'm also back in a Covid bubble, so I can't eat at my favourite little sushi shop near the stadium. I focus on what I want from this trip.

Sometimes you put your hopes and dreams out into the universe – I did that back in 2019 when I verbalised what I was seeking here. It worked that time, and I won my first ever Grand Slam. Subconsciously at least, I'm doing that again now. *Righto, Paris, what are you going to give?* I think to myself. *Are you going to be kind to me, or are you going to break my heart?*

The hallowed French ground of Court Philippe Chatrier really is a beautiful place. It's grown to be one of my favourites. I have a wonderful hit the next day with Svetlana Kuznetsova, one of the best clay-courters I've ever seen. I finish up and tell my physiotherapist, 'This is the best I've felt in a month.' I hit with Naomi Osaka the next day, and feel great again. I'm firing on all cylinders – at least until the 45-minute mark of the session.

When I land after a serve, I feel a dull pain in the top of the hamstring. It doesn't feel quite right, and Naomi doesn't want to do much more anyway, so we cut it short and go inside to see if we can figure out what's happening with my leg. It doesn't feel as bad as I thought out there, so I hit the next day but the pain is there again on my serve – and this time it's worse.

I'm rattled now. I've been doing physio sessions and we've tried to re-create the pain, to get more information, but serving is the only action that flares it up. I walk off court quickly and smash my racquet down on my tennis bag. *I'm meant to be playing in three days!*

I get a scan but it shows little except a little irritation of a nearby muscle and potential bony impingement in the hip joint.

We try something new the next day, taping four different areas of my leg – to the point that I can't fully straighten or bend it. I hit with Storm Sanders, who's just qualified, then I land on a serve and almost fall over, the pain is so intense. Storm knows something isn't right but doesn't say anything. She sits beside me and wraps her arm around me, and I have my head in my hands. My physio then adds more buckles and tape. Now it feels as though I'm preparing for an hour every day just to practise.

The conversation after the session is tough, too. I'm lucky I have a good person with me to talk things through. Her name is Melanie Omizzolo.

I call her my physio but that's selling her short. She's the national physiotherapy manager for Tennis Australia, a role that means she's overseeing the physical wellbeing of a couple of dozen players at any one time. She's been doing that since 2014, which was when I first met her.

Mel and I are both introverts, so we only really interacted then when we had to, but she watched me play qualifiers at Wimbledon that year. Mel sat on a grassy hill there near a court watching me play. She had the impression that I was unhappy. To her, I was that quintessential talented kid, doing something they're good at for all the wrong reasons. She could see it in the way I worked on my recovery, too: I wasn't particularly unprofessional, but nor was I particularly diligent.

After I came back to tennis, and as I got better and started winning more, I saw more and more of Mel. That's not because I was given extra attention, but rather that it's her job to be there throughout those major tournaments on the tour, and to stay until the last Australian is eliminated. The better I got, the more and more often I was the last Aussie to leave tournaments.

Our working relationship quickly became a friendship and I absolutely loved spending time with her.

I came to know her, this girl who grew up in the northern suburbs of Melbourne and went to a Catholic girls' school in Northcote. She was a mad AFL fan, barracked for Carlton and wanted to work in football, as she was fascinated by the process of managing endurance athletes who play a brutal and ballistic contact sport on a weekly basis.

While Mel was completing her post-graduate study, a lecturer took her aside and pointed out that the WTA was looking for physios. Mel replied as only she could or would: 'What's the WTA?' She had no understanding of or interest in tennis, but ended up working for eight years as a contractor physio for the WTA at tour events. Mel had to perform and travel and be independent, and work long hours and get things right.

So yeah, she's exactly the right person to manage me in this moment of pain and uncertainty. The conversation we're having now centres on whether I can still play, and what the risks might be if I decide to try.

'Something doesn't feel right,' Mel says. 'Something doesn't sit right with the pain, with the imaging. We're missing something.'

I can run and walk and play, but not serve, and once I have served I can barely climb a flight of stairs. This injury has come out of nothing, too – just playing against Naomi and landing on a serve like I've landed on a million other serves. In just 48 hours, it's become a major problem.

The results of an ultrasound and an MRI come back, but neither helps with the diagnosis, and the discomfort is only worsening. I'm on heavy painkillers now, and they're barely dulling the sensation. I eventually work out that I can hit a second serve at about half-pace, without using my legs or jumping – a technique that players used 50 years ago, before the start of the power game. But I can't change the entire mechanics of my serve in the space of one day, can I?

By the time I'm ready to walk on court for my first-round match, I have my hamstring taped, my adductor taped, my glute taped and my hip taped – all on the left side. That should get me to the point that I can serve one of those old-timey arm balls with no leg power.

'Tyzz,' I say. 'I'm gonna hit an ace today with a little arm ball.'

He looks unconvinced. 'No, you won't.'

I wink. 'Yeah, I will.'

And I hit an ace early and turn to him and smile, because sometimes you have to find joy in the hard times.

I'm playing against Croatian-born American left-hander Bernarda Pera, and it's brutal out there. The pain increases but I win the first set 6-3. I'm also worried about doing more damage and jeopardising the rest of my season.

I lose the second set but still feel close to winning. I just have to create some pressure, and make Bernarda feel like she has to overplay her shots. That's exactly what happens, and I come off court half-laughing and half-crying.

'How did you do that?' Mel asks. 'I've never seen anything like that in my life.'

I decide I'm going to play the next day, and so we do everything we can. Painkillers. Laser treatment. Ultrasound treatment. I'm now spending two hours a day off court trying to manage my pain and bring it down to an acceptable level. I'm playing Magda Linette, a Polish counterpuncher, and the pain from the start is extreme. My stomach is sore now too, because of the work it's doing to help the other areas, so we tape it up as well. I'm held together by Elastoplast and lose the first set 6-1.

I'm feeling the pain on every serve now, and I'm in danger of completely tearing an abdominal muscle. At 2-2 in the second set, I try to serve normally, and the pain in my leg when I land is so bad I simply buckle over. That's when I walk over to the chair umpire.

She sees my distress. 'Are you okay?'

'Nup,' I answer.

And that's how my 2021 French Open ends. I've run out of time. I take 15 minutes with my team in a treatment room. We don't know what to say. I sit on the floor and put my leg up, because it's the only way to get it free of pain, and I cry – not about the injury but the heartbreak. I have to do media now, and I don't know what I'm going to say. I don't want to look at my phone because I know messages are coming through, and sometimes all that beautiful support only makes the tough times harder.

My team and I sit together, trying to have a laugh. I don't know what lessons or learnings will come of this, and for now at least I don't bother looking for them.

* * *

There are 25 days to Wimbledon and we finally understand what's going on. A ten-centimetre strain deep in my adductor. If I had played any longer in the French Open, Wimbledon would definitely have been ruled out. I'm lucky there is even the slightest possibility.

I give myself some time to be upset. We could have done things differently. In 2019, for instance, I played just 15 matches for the whole year on clay, whereas this year I've played more than 20 before the French Open even began. But there's no point in dwelling on that. If I'm going to dwell on anything, it should be the fact that I've only lost two matches in the past two and a half months. It's been an enjoyable and very successful trip, and you never know what's going to happen next.

The French Open has broken my heart, but I know that Wimbledon can put the pieces back together. A month on grass – I can't wait. We quarantine in London, wait for new scans and figure out a plan for the next three weeks, knowing we have to be ready to overcome setbacks.

We start slowly with rehab in the house we've rented. The only equipment we have access to is a children's swing set so we buy therabands, a watt bike and any other gym gear we can cram into the tiny backyard. We're not far from Wimbledon, and it's lovely. It feels like home. We have a BBQ out the back and a big kitchen. We have cooking competitions – my strength and conditioning man Matt Hayes and me versus Tyzz and Mel – to see who can come up with the best BBQ and salad dinner. It's the first time in months that we're able to cook our own meals on our own schedule.

But in another way, it drives us all mad. Tyzz, Mel, Matt and I are living together in a four-bedroom house, which is close enough quarters at the best of times, but during five days of quarantine it feels as though we're in each other's pockets. We do whatever we can to lighten the mood and keep our nerves from jangling.

I first got to know Matt in 2020, when I was at home a lot and needed someone to train with. He works under Tubs and often works with the younger kids, and I hadn't been home enough to get to know him, but I quickly saw that he's very good at what he does.

He slots in like he's been one of us forever. I like him, too. He's a sports tragic, loves his AFL and NRL – the Brisbane Lions and the Brisbane Broncos. We're compatible as co-workers, able to slip out of easy conversation and jokes ('Ash, I'll get a tattoo if you win this Grand Slam') and into the discipline required. He communicates well when he isn't sure about something, and is firm with me when he is.

I need that certainty right now, because this injury cloud is forcing me to do things differently. Matt comforts me with his grand '21-day plan' that will take us through to that first Monday of Wimbledon. He has me walking up and down the stairs to activate my hip. I buy a kids' scooter and, in our large house, I start scooting from room to room, building the load through my left leg. Childlike and fun – just how I like it.

Jumping is the hardest part. I'm terrified of landing after a serve. *I don't know if I'm ready for this*, I worry. *This movement I've been making for 20 years now brings on the most extraordinary pain of my career.*

We start by hopping, as if skipping over a crack in the footpath. A bilateral hop feels okay too, and then a small jump, but I'm favouring my right side. I'm terrified to go through the full motion on my left, but Matty encourages me.

'I don't think I'm ready!' I say. 'It's going to hurt!'

He keeps telling me just to give it a try.

Jump. Land. *PAIN*. Straightaway. 'Nup, I'm done,' I say.

Eventually we're freed from quarantine – but rather than go our separate ways, we go out together, down to the local pub for a Sunday beef roast, and Yorkshire pudding.

I tell Mel I don't want to know the detailed results of the new scan. I trust her implicitly and I want to go by feel. I want to treat the symptoms. All I want to know from the medical team is whether the strain is a bit better than it was.

Even so, I'm scared ahead of the results.

For most of our time in quarantine, I had taken myself to bed early, trying to give myself space to think about what might happen. Little did I know, Mel, Matt and Tyzz were all just as concerned. Deep down, they knew how unlikely our Wimbledon dream was.

The scan results arrive one night while I'm in bed curled up with *The Final Hour* by Tom Wood. I don't learn the outcome until the morning.

'It's better,' Mel tells me. 'It's improved.'

Time to crack on then, and get down to the All England Club. I call Mum straightaway to deliver the good news.

Matt's making sure we stick to the plan. 'We are going to have a setback. We're going to have something that comes up,' he says. 'You're going to wake up sore in the morning, so we need to monitor what's happening.'

Next I'll try to serve, and I'm nervous. We decide to literally *walk* through the serve, with me keeping both feet on the ground and just rolling my arm over. I hit five or six that way and it feels fine.

'Can I try a little jump serve?' I ask Mel. 'Maybe 25 per cent effort?'

'Yeah, yeah,' she says. 'Try it.'

And in that moment, we all hold our breath. The serve is pain-free.

'Nice,' says Mel. 'Do it again.'

I serve another handful, and Mel cautions me: 'Just do ten serves – no more.'

I want to do more. I want to hit my serve at 50 per cent – even just once or twice.

Mel finally gives in to my whingeing. I can hit 15 serves at an easy half-strength swing. I feel no pain and smile, but now we're nearing the start of Wimbledon and the stress is mine, because I know that if I'm going to compete – to have any chance of winning – I need to be at my peak, and I haven't even reached 75 per cent of my capacity.

Now it's the week before Wimbledon and I feel ready to play a practice set.

We move into a hotel near Westminster that has about 2000 rooms, and I'm going to be in one of these for a while – depending on how far I go in this tournament. If I win, it could be 23 days going back and forth from this place. This doesn't feel like Wimbledon to me. It's unique, and challenging, and a good reason to remind myself of my motto for 2021: *Spirit of adventure*.

It's now two days before the tournament begins, and I'm finally allowed to hit a serve at 100 per cent – for two service games only, no more and no less. I'm all set. I'm about to embark on a two-week journey against the best players in the world, and I haven't raised a sweat on court in a month.

Today, Love Won

The night before Wimbledon, I don't feel stressed or excited. I feel present – existing fully in the moment as night falls on London. I am ready in the most calm and composed way possible. And then I try to sleep.

Normally I fall into bed early because I tend to rise early, but tonight, sleep just won't come. I roll onto my side and my back and my front, looking for the perfect posture, searching out the warmest pocket under the sheets and the cool side of the pillow, but nothing feels right.

I tap Garry on the shoulder. 'Are you still awake?'

He sniffs and yawns. 'Yeah, what's up?'

'I'm terrified.'

'What do you mean?'

'I'm terrified that I'm going to lose tomorrow,' I say. 'And I'm terrified that I'm going to win tomorrow.'

All that peace and confidence I had been so proud of all day are gone now in the darkness. For the first time in my life, I am scared by the outcome of a tennis match.

Garry turns to me. 'It doesn't matter,' he says, opening his half-shut eyes and smiling. 'Just play.'

I need to hear these words. I need to hear that what happens on court won't matter to him, or to anyone else in my family.

We both roll over into fitful sleep, but before we do, he hammers the point home one more time.

'Just go and win it,' he says. 'And if you don't, it doesn't matter.'

Garry and I met five years earlier, in late 2016, at the Brookwater Golf and Country Club – my local track. It's a great course, and new, too. And for 12 years this was Garry's office.

He spent his days here doing a traineeship as a golf pro, while also working as an irrigation technician. He loves grass, and gardens. He has a bizarre love for every blade. He's the one who takes the time even now to tend to our own lawns. He has three garage cabinets filled with fertilisers and treatments.

Garry was born in Gladstone, way up the coast from me, somewhere between Bundy (Bundaberg) and Rocky (Rockhampton), but he grew up close, in Ipswich. My sister Ali's husband went to school with him, so we knew some of the same people, and trod some of the same territory, although we never crossed paths.

We met through the golf club, both playing. I found him to be instantly authentic and genuine. He's funny, too. Garry is that guy who makes people laugh.

Our early days dating were as stress-free as it gets. We went out a few times, and then I went away to Europe on tour for 12 weeks. That meant we ended up getting to know one another through messages and phone calls in different time zones. It was a different way to start a relationship, but nothing we've ever done has been normal.

We knew each other so well before we spent any real time together in person, but it was still nice to get to know him up close and personal, and to discover all his quirks. To learn that he's a big softie – but with an incredibly short fuse. To see him carry himself with strength – but then lose his mind howling in pain when he stubs his toe.

I knew he had never been interested in tennis, but I quickly learnt how little he knew. He didn't watch tennis. Didn't like tennis. Didn't understand the rules of tennis. The game had no meaning to him – and I liked that. In truth, I needed that. It shouldn't matter so much, but it seemed crucial in my mind that my partner be interested in me in spite of tennis and not because of it, and that was Garry. He's been with me since I had only just picked up a racquet again, when I was unranked. He loved me for me, and became the most important cog in the second phase of my career.

Garry threw himself into the deep end, too. He never seemed worried or concerned by the time I was spending away, and never pushed or insisted I cut anything back. I knew instantly that what mattered to me mattered to him. He would watch all of my matches, no matter where I was playing, no matter whether it meant sitting up late, alone in front of a flatscreen or squinting in the sunshine somewhere, trying to follow a live stream on his phone screen.

And afterwards, he was always the first person to message me, win or lose.

He had no problem being at my beck and call either.

'Can you fly here tomorrow?' I might ask. 'I really need you.'

'No worries,' he would reply.

I dragged him into a completely different world, but he handled it all.

He quickly became someone I could turn to in my darkest moments – the one who would always make me laugh. One of the worst moments of my life on tour came on a day when something between us – our harmony – broke.

I was playing in the Italian Open in Rome in 2019, and Garry was scheduled to fly home halfway through the tournament, as he had work commitments. As it happened, his departure date was at the same time as my match against Kristina Mladenovic.

The person I loved the most was leaving, at the very moment I was playing. I was supposed to be studying the tall French doubles specialist on the other side of the net, monitoring her heavy serve, but all I could picture was Garry in a cab, Garry at the airport, Garry on a plane, and me left here alone. I couldn't focus. I was crying on the court, and once I got off the court, my tears were out of control. Tyzz was a little confused that he couldn't calm me down.

I called Crowey.

'Ash,' he said, pausing. 'You're a lover. And you're a fighter. But today, love won.'

Garry made his own sacrifices, too. Anyone who's in a relationship with a professional athlete does. At the end of 2019, for instance, he deferred doing his PGA traineeship so he could follow me on the tennis tour more in 2020. Of course, Covid changed the entire world in early 2020, but I loved the fact that he wanted to be with me and share the journey of my career. He found a new love later with caddying, and is pursuing that now. The young golfer he's working with, Louis Dobbelaar, is still at the start of his career and is due to begin his PGA journey soon, but I love watching those two work together. It reminds me a lot of my relationship with my team, and I know it'll be a partnership that lasts.

One of Garry's best traits is that he uses whatever he has to help people succeed. He never interfered in anything when it came to tennis, and not all partners are able to do that. Whether it was the business side of the Barty brand or the tennis decisions of Team Ash, he left it to others, understanding the value of an expert. I love that about him – if he doesn't know something, he says so, and never tries to bluff his way through. That's an honourable characteristic in a person.

In 2021, when he arrived in London and entered the tournament bubble at Wimbledon, it had been three months since I'd seen him. It was always our plan for him to join us at Wimbledon, but I didn't realise how much of a positive impact it would have on me. The environment can be intense, and filled with stresses, and everyone needs someone to lean on. I wanted someone to talk to about my injured leg – or, when my mood changed, to *not* talk about my injured leg. For the team, Garry was a fresh face and brought a new energy.

I love what we've built together. I love that when Liverpool is playing, I know Garry will be wearing one of his 50-odd jerseys. I love that if I give him any chance at all to control the sound system at home, DJ Dillon Francis will be blaring. I love that when we're near an In-N-Out Burger in the United States, I can guarantee that he'll be popping in to get a 'double double' with fries. I love that he's compassionate and tolerant but has no patience at all for people who lie or who don't do what they say they're going to do. I love that – as a Queenslander – Garry's sporting hero could be anyone from Adam Scott to Allan Border, Mick Doohan to Mal Meninga, but he fell the hardest for the hardest hitter: left-handed opening batsman Matthew Hayden. I love that Garry's dogs and my dogs – our dogs – are the most important thing in his day, most of the time even more than me. I love that he sits on the steps with my youngest nephew and talks dinosaurs until the kid is exhausted, and that if Lucy wants to kick a ball she only needs to look in his direction. He has always fitted into our family and has never changed who he is. That's what I love the most.

Triumph and Disaster

Wimbledon is the tournament that everybody knows. Even if you don't know that the playing surface is comprised of 54 million plants, each cut to a precise 8 millimetres high, you understand that there's something special about the surface. And whether or not you know the exact clothing rules, you probably know that all players here wear all white.

Winning Wimbledon also means immortality. No one forgets what happens here. They celebrate and welcome past champions in the most special way, so you aren't just a winner here, you're in its very history. The trophies have never changed, and the honour boards are displayed around the grounds. You feel surrounded by those names – watched by them. As a kid, you think, *I can't be one of those*. It's like thinking, *One day I'll be an astronaut*, or *When I grow up I want to be prime minister*. It feels impossible.

I've known for a long time that if I were to succeed here, I would be satisfied with my journey.

* * *

It's late June 2021. The London weather is awful and I really don't want to practise today. I don't want to hinder my leg or my hip. I don't want to deal with the traffic and the hassle.

Jamie Baker, the tournament director, sends me a message: *Ash, we would love you to open up Centre Court on Tuesday at 1.30 pm.* That changes my mood, lightening me up, until I realise why I've been chosen. Simona Halep, my good mate and the reigning champion, sends me a message too. She's woken up with back spasms and can't get out of bed without help. Centre Court was hers to open, and now her Wimbledon defence has ended before it's even begun.

I don't feel I deserve this position, and I'm unsure of my body, too. I'm playing against Carla Suárez Navarro, and I know this is her last Wimbledon.

'I've never played her,' I say to Tyzz, 'and with everything she's gone through …'

She retired when she was diagnosed with Hodgkin's lymphoma, and two years later has come back to play.

'I don't know how to feel.' *Should I feel excited?* I wonder. *Scared?* I promise myself I will at least smile when walking onto court. I have good reason.

I ask Mel not to tape me as much as usual because – for the first time in my life – I care a great deal about what I'm wearing.

I have a special outfit for this tournament. In early 2020, Nikki and I had noted that Wimbledon 2021 would be the 50th anniversary of Evonne's first victory here. We thought recreating her iconic scalloped white dress would be meaningful. I had looked through a variety of designs from Fila and chosen a shortlist, then asked my niece Lucy to narrow down the selections and make my final pick.

I had called Evonne and asked if I could wear a dress inspired by her, and she was taken aback and said yes. Deep down, I don't think she was ever going to say no, but I needed her permission all the same.

Unveiling it on Centre Court is too big a moment to ruin with a bunch of medical tape.

I'm in the hallway now, waiting to be welcomed into the public arena, and I see words in front of me. It's from Rudyard Kipling's poem 'If'. The poem is placed where the players at Wimbledon can see it before they begin their match:

If you can meet with Triumph and Disaster

And treat those two 'imposters' just the same ...

If you haven't read the poem in full, it's worth doing. Every line speaks to me. The messages are clear to me. Keep your head. Trust yourself. Don't hate or think yourself wiser than others. Dream, without letting those dreams become your master. Be ready to win or lose. Stay true to your roots. If you can do all that, the poem says, 'Yours is the earth, and everything that's in it.'

Yep, I think, *let's play some tennis*.

We do, but of course it rains. I stand with Carla while they close the roof, and we talk like practice partners. I win the first set, lose the second because I'm being too passive, and then flick a switch in the third set to end it. At least I'm off the mark and over the hump.

The next morning, I roll over in bed and I know I'm going to be sore, but it's not too bad. By the afternoon I can't bend over and touch my toes to do up my shoelaces. I can't sit on a chair because my glutes are so sore. My very light practice session with Tyzz is a funny disaster. We laugh and accept that it's more about recovery now – we won't stress over the tennis.

My second-round match is against Anna Blinkova. I know it's a match I can win while going through the motions, but my body is seriously hurting. I can barely push off to serve, and when I do, I can't find the court. But I find a way to win, and then I collapse in agony at the hotel.

A couple of days later, I work myself into my third-round clash in similar fashion, trying to take it up a level against Kateřina Siniaková.

I'm aching, but my body feels as though it's finding its routine now. Long-distance runners talk about pain in this way. The lactic acid builds up in their legs earlier in most races than many people would think. And their lungs are on fire quickly too. They talk about 'settling in with the suffering'.

My team asks me time and time again, 'How are you feeling? Do you have pain?'

Nothing.

Let's go.

My opponent in the fourth round is Barbora Krejčíková, an all-court, accurate and aggressive player. She has just won the French Open.

I want this match-up badly. I feel that dark desire taking hold – the mongrel inside of me. I want to prove something to myself, but also to everyone else. *I'm better than her – she's not beating me today.*

She makes me uncomfortable early, but I find a way to read her patterns and win the games that matter most. On match point, I offer a massive fist-pump to my team, and walk off court with purpose.

'Man,' I say to Tyzz, 'I wanted that.'

He nods. 'Oh, I could tell.'

It's getting closer now, my goal. It's 2021, three years since the Kasatkina meltdown, and three years since I met Crowey. I've been keeping a journal.

I write in it every day, and I also write down goals at the start of every year. It makes me accountable. Sometimes the goals are specific and sometimes they're general.

In 2020, one of my specific goals was to make the quarter-finals at Wimbledon. Then in mid-2020 I did an interview with wheelchair athlete Kurt Fearnley, and he's easy-going and disarming and so without realising it, I said to him that I wanted to win Wimbledon. No one had heard me say that before, because I don't think I'd ever said it before, even to myself. But it had escaped from my lips, so at the beginning of 2021 I made it a firm target. 'Win Wimbledon' was the primary goal.

Next, it's me and Ajla Tomljanović – Aussie against Aussie. I can't even imagine the buzz back home.

I tell myself I want to play a stand-out match. I want to be respectful but assertive. In reality, this means too much to me to think like this. If I'm honest, I want to make Ajla feel tiny, thinner than a blade of grass. I want to use my experience playing on Centre Court and in Grand Slam finals to make her feel as though she doesn't belong.

And that's what I do. I find the openings and drive the dagger in. It's a 6-1, 6-3 win. I couldn't allow the fact that she is Australian to factor into my thinking at all.

My semi-final is against Angelique Kerber, whom I haven't played in a long time, and who has a winning record against me. I've always felt forced to go a little above myself to match her experience, and this year I believe she is the one to beat.

I play close to the best tennis of my life against Kerber. *CALM, CLEAR, PRESENT, CONFIDENT & SHARP*. My legs are burning the entire match and my energy is flagging, but I settle in with my suffering. When you walk off the court with a win after working so hard, the feeling is unlike anything else.

'I can't do that again,' I say to Tyzz. 'That's as good as it gets for me.' I'm into the final at Wimbledon.

* * *

It rains all morning. We have a little bit of time before our warm-up, so we wander over to a vacant gym, and Tyzz sees a small sponge tennis ball, while Garry finds a broom handle. We may as well kill time with a cricket match. Our pitch is the open-plan treatment area. Mel is trying to warm me up and treat me, but I can't do it.

'It's my innings,' I plead. 'They've gotta bowl me out first.'

The gym supervisor raises an eyebrow when she finds us, but there's news at least. I can have a practice hit on Court 1 ... alongside my opponent. This has never been done before. Finalists in the greatest Grand Slam of all do not warm up next to one another on the morning of their match. They're like a bride and groom on the day of their wedding – kept apart until the last moment.

Yet here we are, me hitting with Tyzz, and Karolína (Kaya) Plíšková hitting with her coach. Tyzz and I are both wearing coloured clothes, because I wasn't planning to practise on a match court. This simply isn't allowed at Wimbledon. But due to the last-minute change, the All England Club allows us to play – just this once. But I'm embarrassed. Mortified, really.

Kaya and I are quite good friends, and we have a laugh about it all – and then a dozen cameras pop up, but they're late to the party. It's time for us to warm up, get changed and get ready.

As I walk out onto Centre Court for the final, I do what I always do. Look up and smile.

The roof is open – this is good for me. Kaya's biggest weapon is her serve. If the roof is closed and she can launch at me all day with no gusts of wind or bursts of sunshine to throw her off, I'll be in trouble.

I win the toss and elect to serve. I always do. Give me the responsibility straightaway. My first service game is as good as I could have asked for. *Bang, bang, bang*, I think. *Yep, good.*

We expect Kaya to serve hard and fast in response, but the first one she sends down is slow and tentative. *Why?*

I look at her face and see something there. Kaya's nervous – and that relaxes me. I look at my box and smile. Tyzz has noticed it too.

When you're playing tennis, you're also playing mind games. All players have 'tells' that reveal how they're feeling about their place in the match. Right now, I read Kaya's face and sense a lack of energy. I know I can take control here.

She usually comes out on fire and I build into matches, but today she's so slow that I don't need to do much to win the first four games. My big focus is to take away her aces and easy points. I can't let her establish any flow. I power through the first set, 6-3. She doesn't hit a single ace.

In the second set she changes her serving spots and

it puts me in a bind. I can't cover both edges of the box, and she's stretching me on either side. She picks her spots well and finds her way back into the match. My legs are tiring now and I'm shaking a little. Now we feel on equal footing. Now I just need to focus.

I walk as slowly as I can between points, trying to get oxygen into my limbs. It's 5-5 when I finally break her serve – she's 40-15 up and I have no right to win it, but I dig and dig and dig and it falls my way. Then I serve for the match, and she has no right to win it but she digs and digs and digs and finds a way to break back. We're both playing elite tennis. We're going to a third set.

I'm going to win this match, I think. *I'm gonna find a way. This is mine. I want it more than her.*

My heart beats quicker now, but my thoughts remain clear. *She's going to have to work for every single point.*

The crowd is incredible, but it's not their fight – this is me against her. At the heart of a match like this lies the question: *What do I have to do to beat that girl down the other end of the court?*

I don't remember the last point, but I'm told Kaya hits a backhand into the bottom of the net, and the spectators rise with an almighty roar. That sound rushes through me.

Is this happening? I think. *Can this be real?*

I cover my face and sink to my knees. I quickly hug Kaya and I forget to thank James Keothavong for umpiring the match – I later feel awful for this. I toss my racquet down and drop my head and crouch on the court once again, as though I'm simply not ready to open up to all the warmth and rapture raining down on Centre Court. My left leg almost buckles underneath me, and I look up with mist in my eyes. *What has just happened?* I thank the crowd but I know I need to get to my team.

I go straight to my box, thinking I'll climb up into it. At first I go the wrong way, and then the fans point me in the right direction to find them. I wrap

Mel in my arms, and Matty next, and then Garry. I sink my head into his shoulder, smudging his shirt with my tears.

'This is so embarrassing,' I whisper. 'I'm crying in front of millions of people.'

I hold Tyzz next, and I love the look on his face – a mix of pride and belief. I give one final hug to Stormy, a doubles partner who has been there with me through thick and thin. I am so glad she is there to share this moment with us.

During the presentation, I'm nervous. I try not to pay attention to the glow of celebrity or the glare of the public eye. I also know that David Beckham and Benedict Cumberbatch and Sienna Miller have been in these stands. Watching this final are Prince William and the Duchess of Cambridge, Kate Middleton, who's presenting the trophy to me.

After the ceremony comes the traditional balcony presentation, but first I'm asked to walk through and briefly speak to those who were sitting in the royal box. Kate's smiling and so is William, and I have no idea what to say.

That balcony moment is one I will never forget. A view that deserves to be a postcard – a sea of people, and my favourite lush green courts quietly resting in the background. Amazing.

The photographs are done, and the officials come to take the trophy away. And I finally get to see my team.

'I've just cried everywhere on international television,' I say to Tyzz. 'I don't remember what I've said in the last five minutes.'

I open my phone and see messages from my family and friends. Everything rested on process and mindset and belief. *CALM, CLEAR, PRESENT, CONFIDENT & SHARP.*

Now I finally feel able to ask Mel to tell me about my injury in detail. The strain was still there, she tells me. It had improved, but only a little.

'You still had a ten-centimetre strain, which should have kept you out of competition altogether, and this is why we held you back,' she says. 'Bad luck that you were grumpy with us for the first week, but we did what we had to do.'

I can't believe what I'm hearing. I'll owe Mel, Tyzz and Matt forever. *How did we even get on the court?*

I have a few hours of press commitments ahead of me now, and it's 4.30 am in Australia, but it's my first chance to talk to Nikki and Crowey. They're two of the best phone calls of my life.

The All England Club organises a private dinner for my team – a beautiful five-course meal that is way too fancy for us. I'm overlooking the River Thames and realise that I haven't called Mum. I FaceTime her now, and I cry and she cries and everyone else does too. My body is wrecked and my heart is exhausted.

Our exhausted and emotional celebrations end early, and I drift off to sleep and fall into my dreams, one unreality meeting another.

The Last Summer

A new summer comes and the idea of slaving in the sun and hitting a few thousand tennis balls and going from home to car to airport to hotel to practice court over and over again has never felt so pointless.

Today I start with my favourite hard 30-minute bike session: five sets of a four-minute time trial, then two minutes of rest. Usually I love it. Today, I quit the session during the second rep. Something I have never done before. This sounds like a little thing, but it's not – it's a clear red flag. Pre-season training is always a slog but there's a rhythm, too, where the hard work turns into something you eat up. This isn't that, though.

Soon I begin cracking jokes – 'Think this'll be my last summer, guys' – and people laugh, because they think it couldn't be true. *She couldn't quit, as the number 1 player in the world and reigning Wimbledon champion, could she?*

A normal practice hit in our first week back is 60–90 minutes long. Ben, Nikki's husband, knows that my coordination returns more quickly than for other players, and that he doesn't have to overplay me. He tells me that Tyzz is always secretly happy when Ben takes over that first week of pre-season hitting, because he knows I'll be in a bad mood while I'm rusty.

Ben thinks he knows why, too. When I've had a break and come back and start hitting tennis balls, I have to start getting my head around the oncoming year. The tour becomes a reality.

Ben's known me for a long time. He played a lot as a junior and was good, but he stopped at 15 to live as a normal kid.

He met me when I was just 13. I was at the national academy, and he was looking after the elite boys from Queensland.

Ben was the chaperone on my first overseas playing trip, to New Zealand. I got homesick quickly on that tour and he saw that immediately. We had spent enough time together talking sports trash with one another, arguing over whose rugby league team was better, for him to spot that my spark was missing.

These days, Ben is one of those people who makes training days fun. We have the silliest arguments, about whether BBQ sauce or tomato sauce is better – and the debate never ends in a win. (Although tomato sauce is clearly better.)

Ben calls me out and challenges me, even though he knows I hate being called out and challenged.

That honesty is a two-way street, however, and

so now, facing a new pre-season, I go down to his and Nikki's house in Runaway Bay. Ostensibly I'm there to do some signings – posters and hats. It's late morning and I'm sitting in his office signing, and then I'm venting, and before I know it the whole truth comes tumbling out of me.

'I don't know what I'm playing for anymore,' I say. 'I think I'm done.'

'Yeah, I get it,' he replies. 'But to be honest, you haven't won a hardcourt Slam yet.'

There's a silence, and he's the one to fill it first. 'I think if you were to go racquets down right now,' he says, 'there would be something hanging over your head – there would be unfinished business.'

'Benny, I've got nothing left, no spark.'

'But you don't have an Australian Open, and you want one,' he says, winking, poking the bear. 'Just go and win the Aussie Open. And then retire.'

I'm quiet after that. I don't like this conversation. I especially don't like that he's right.

Win one and then stop. I can do that, I think. *Set me a challenge? Fine. Game on.*

* * *

I play the final in the Adelaide International and take the title for the second time. *Yay*, I think limply. *I guess?*

I don't know how to explain this new attitude, but I think of it as careless: I know I'm about to quit the game, so I know the next big loss is the last loss. Crowey doesn't call it careless, though. He calls it carefree. I may not feel the excitement to play matches or the thrill of the fight, but I'm also without any distraction or distress. People in my team keep asking, 'Is she okay? Are you okay, Ash?' – and I am more than okay. I'm dialled in to the task at hand.

We head to the Australian Open and I'm reading more crime books, and having the odd BBQ with steak or chicken from the local butcher and a bunch of veggies or salad from the supermarket, and I'm looking forward to playing.

Usually I'm jangled by now, reliving my history in this tournament, which is filled with regret. But none of it troubles me as much as it once did.

In my opening match I'll be playing a qualifier, so I look through the list of who that might be. There's only one name that makes me pause: Lesia Tsurenko. I've lost to her previously. I just want a comfortable match-up, and would prefer to avoid her, but of course that's who I draw.

She's coming off an injury, but she's tricky and she does that thing I hate, putting a lot of balls in awkward places. She doesn't so much dominate as frustrate.

We play in the Rod Laver Arena. But it's over in 50 minutes. Do I need a physio? Nup. Just home for a sleep, ready for the next round.

I've never played Lucia Bronzetti before, and never watched her play. I see her at the coin toss, and although she's 22 she looks 17, and I can tell she's intimidated. She has nothing that can hurt me, and it's over in 57 minutes.

On my day off, I go for a walk with Crowey and his spanador, Molly, and we talk about how this is it for me – and how I need everyone to accept that.

'I'm not going to regret this,' I tell him. 'I'm tired of people telling me I can play one or two tournaments a year, that I can do Wimbledon and the Australian Open and avoid all the others. I *can't* pick and choose, because there's all the work in between.' I don't want to train for six months just to play a few rounds at a Slam, and then do it all again. I'm done.

He understands and he gives me a hug. This is the end, the line in the sand, and now everyone knows for sure.

I play Camila Giorgi in the third round, and I like this match-up. She's very structured, and smacks the ball hard. But I can get the ball up, and down, and change the pace, and loop it, and constantly change her contact point. Her pace doesn't bother me either – I can use that against her.

There's all this extra hype, as usual at a Grand Slam, but we muffle that with silly games in our warm-up. I've got some tape so we draw a little net on the wall and start playing soccer. We play cricket, too.

I'm up against Amanda Anisimova in the fourth round, which is a shock to some, because the media has been talking all week about the prospect of me playing Naomi Osaka, but Naomi loses and I'm annoyed that Amanda hasn't been respected.

'You guys always predict this stuff will happen,' I tell the press. 'But it *never* happens.'

Tyzz offers me his notes about Amanda's damaging first-serve speed, and tricky second-serve location. She likes to return through the middle, he says, and if I go wide to her backhand it needs to be with quality.

'You need to expose her movement,' he says, 'because any time she's able to establish a good position on the ball, she's dangerous.'

The last thing Tyzz tells me before any match is about attitude. This is what he texts me: *Must be ready to compete in this one. She's gonna be up and about after beating Naomi. Look to stick to your plans.*

It feels like a dangerous match but it's over in an hour and 15 minutes, straight sets again.

Tick, move on. *I'm into the quarters but I've done nothing*, I think. *I haven't needed to do anything.*

The quarter-finals continue the theme of the tournament so far. I'm up against Jess Pegula, whose billionaire father owns NFL club the Buffalo Bills.

I start well, and Jess completely hands me the match. This match falls into her too-hard basket and is done in 63 minutes. Afterwards, she admits as much, telling the media she felt 'helpless' out there.

'When she gets into a rhythm, she can kind of run away,' Jess says about me. 'It doesn't feel good.'

I've played six matches in barely more than six hours all up, and I'm into the semi-finals. At the beginning of the fortnight, for something different and to completely lighten up, I begin doing something now that I never do – I listen to the outside world.

* * *

A couple of years ago, Crowey told me a story about Cathy Freeman and the 2000 Sydney Olympic Games. She was asked at a press conference how she was dealing with the pressure, and her answer was simple: 'I'm not.' Every journalist in the room perked up after that comment, thinking a story was breaking about an athlete about to crack under the strain, but then Cathy clarified what she meant: 'I'm not dealing with the pressure, because it's not even entering my attention.'

But now I'm going a different way. The TV is usually on mute, but now I crank up the volume.

I begin listening to the media, curious about what they think they know about me. *They're analysing but have no idea what's happening,* I realise. *And no idea what I'm feeling.* They only see me on court, when I'm not even really there. They see me at press conferences, too, when I'm never going to tell them anything, yet they think I'm revealing all.

For a few years now, Garry and I have been playing a game. Whenever we're watching TV or listening to the radio and someone says my name, we let out a little 'Woo!' and do a high-five. (Watching the morning news at the wrong time of year can make your hand sore.) We take it to a new level at the 2022 Australian Open, starting a new team WhatsApp group called 'Where's Ash?' The rule is simple: if you spot my image or name in any context, send in a picture, draw a face on it, have fun with it.

Soon the photos start rolling in. Me on bus stops and tram stops and train station platforms. Someone sees my name on the news ticker crawling across the bottom of a television at JB Hi-Fi. There I am on a skyscraper in the city.

A strange thing happens, too – I begin to understand that I'm not playing for me anymore. I'm playing for everyone else. I'm playing for my team. For this country.

The semi-final is against Maddie Keys, whom I love. I'm happy if this is as far as my tournament goes. *If I lose to Maddie, that's okay*, I think, *because I'd be genuinely happy for her to get into a Grand Slam final.*

Tyzz gives me his instructions, and I go out on court and perform as instructed. That's the way it works in Slams, of course. You need all your advice up front because there's no direct coaching allowed on court. You can look at your box and, mostly, I look to Tyzz for reassurance.

I don't look at him at all in this semi-final – in fact, I haven't all tournament. Right now it's just me and Maddie, and then when match point falls my way it's just me, with a single fist-pump for company. I'm into the final of the Australian Open.

Who I'll be playing against is decided the next day. Iga Świątek is playing Danielle Collins, and for me the equation is simple. I love Iga, and I have a rocky relationship with Danielle. I want to play Iga. I want to share it with her. But Danielle wins, and I think back to the matches we've had in the past and how they were never fun. I never walk off court after playing Danielle thinking, *That was good tennis*. Each match has been an ugly, tiring fight.

Tyzz texts me his long strategy, and I scroll through it, trying to remember a few important points, but it's always the emotional notes that I remember best. *She is weird, and hard to read, but is vulnerable when up in the score, and definitely guilty of getting a little bit tight*, Tyzz writes. *At times, when feeling anxious, she will lose composure and get angry and loud.*

Danielle enters the arena first, while I wait at the top of the stairs. The crowd is restless, the murmuring audible even to me in the shadows. I make a promise to myself – *Look up and take it all in, and walk out with a smile*, because wearing a smile onto the court is what I've done since I was a little girl. It's my way of reminding myself to have fun. I do the coin toss, and consider it my duty to make the kid flipping the coin smile and laugh, and then I feel settled.

Things mostly go smoothly in the first set. Danielle had a small opportunity in one of my service games but I hit a big second serve, find my forehand with the first ball and pull it inside in – my go-to pattern when it matters. That gets the game back to deuce, and I play two more solid points to win. Holding my serve is massive for me. I win the first set 6-3, rounding it out with an ace. *Yep*, I think, nodding. *This is good.*

But in the second set I get a little passive and things start to go south. My slice is no longer crisply chipped. My powerful first serve is a little loose. I run to the wrong places. I double-fault. Danielle has court position and is controlling the centre. She's crunching second serves and being assertive early in rallies. Before I can blink I'm down 1-5. How do I get back in this contest?

Crowey always says that in such moments you draw down on your values. I think of a few words that take me back to my earliest times in tennis: 'Happy', 'Excited', 'Loved'. How do I stay calm under pressure? I try to remember the little girl who fell in love with the game.

There is a moment in the second set that snaps me back into the right place. Danielle breaks to lead 5-1, turns to her team and screams, 'Come on!' It's loud – very loud. It's the first time she really tries to assert any positive energy into the match. I'm a little confused as to why she chooses this moment, as she's all over me. It's unnecessary. The crowd sense this and get a little fired up. I smile and think, *Game on*.

That won't get me back into this match entirely, though, so I also call to mind the tactics Tyzz has drilled into me. I can see that he wants this one badly – for him, for me, for us – so I forget none of his tips and fundamentals.

Find forehands, I think. *Find forehands and be aggressive.*

I know in this moment, too, that this is the only match of the summer where I will not be able to accept a loss. I can't accept losing to her here and now. I won't. It's not an option.

Find your feet. Find forehands. Be aggressive. Every point.

I tell myself that if there's a ball that I'd hit with a backhand 65 per cent of the time, I'll run around and hit it with a forehand – and I'll do that again and again and again. Why? Because if Danielle looks over the net and sees me hitting forehand after forehand, she'll think she's doing something wrong. She'll think she needs to do something different – something *extra* – and that's when she'll make a mistake.

We go to 3-5 and I can see her wavering now. The crowd is as loud as I've ever heard them. We get to 5-5, and I can feel the control spilling back my way. Danielle looks unnerved as she holds serve. Then it's 6-6 and we're going to a tie-breaker – but the momentum is all mine. She's vulnerable. She's tightening. She's angry.

For the first half of the tie-breaker, I'm playing into the wind. *Make her earn every point,* I think.

First point, she serves and we get into a rally, but she's impatient and presses too hard for an advantage, and her forehand goes long. 1-0.

Second point, I serve, and fault. I put heavy topspin on my second serve, and just a fraction quicker than normal, and it cramps her left hip. She gets aggressive and doesn't respect it enough, and misses her backhand return long. 2-0.

Third point, I hit my go-to serve and she makes the return but I work hard to find a forehand and the court is open for my inside-out forehand. She doesn't get near it. *Bang*. 3-0.

Now the tie-breaker is different.

Fourth point, she serves and I find a short slice backhand return that is just *nasty*. It gets me in the rally, and when I get the second slice I place it short and low, because I know that with Danielle's forehand grip she can't do damage when the ball is below her knees. The slice forces her down and in, and all she can offer is a cross-court forehand. I drop my reply over the net, and she flicks it high to buy herself some time. I hit a routine smash into the open court and the crowd goes nuts. 4-0. I give them a little fist-pump.

Fifth point, she serves and I miss the return, barely connecting with the racquet.

Sixth point, I'm serving again, and with my second serve I go slow and high into the wind. It catches her off-guard and so she smothers it, dumping the ball into the net. There's something about the way the arena cheers now – I can almost hear every guttural bellow and squeal.

I've lost track of the score but I don't want to look up at the scoreboard because I know the eyes of everyone inside Rod Laver Arena are on me, not to mention the 4,261,000 people watching at home. I sneak a quick glance to check as we change ends. 5-1.

Seventh point, I have the wind behind me now, and all of Australia too. She presses with a double-handed backhand hard and flat, and my return is long. 5-2.

Eighth point, she serves and pushes hard in the long rally that follows. I use my defensive slice, and *then* use my slice low and slow down the middle. It's a ball she thinks she can hurt me with, but she doesn't adjust to the pace and is way too early on it. She shanks it wide. 6-2.

Ninth point. Match point. Championship point. *No cheapies. Get yourself into the point.*

Danielle goes for a big free winner, a flat serve down the T, but I love this because there's no risk, and I can chip that ball back just past the service line. She rips a backhand cross-court and I use my slice. It's not the big deep slice that gives me time, but the short slice that brings her in, taking her away from the baseline. She wants to control the point from the back of the court, but I've forced her to approach. Now she only has one option – my forehand – and it leaves her as a sitting duck.

I see my spot, my favourite shot, the cross-court winner, and there is no hesitation. I don't nurse it, I *crunch* it – and as soon as I do, I know exactly where it's going to land. I know it's going past her, and that she'll barely get her racquet up to swing. I don't even bother recovering for the next shot because I know the ball isn't coming back. I take one step and spin on my heels, turning to my box, and it's all over. 7-2. I've won the 2022 Australian Open.

I'm screaming now, letting everything out, flexing my forearms and roaring again and again. I'm aware that my hands are sweaty, and in that moment the world is vibrating. I forget my surroundings. Have I shaken the umpire's hand? Have I thanked the crowd? Have I put my gear away? I don't know what I've done or what I'm supposed to do. Casey is at the side of the court and I run to hug her first. 'Thank God you're here,' I say. 'I love you.'

Evonne presenting me the Daphne Akhurst Memorial Cup is one of the best surprises and one of my favourite moments. My dear friend, my mentor and my family. It couldn't have been more perfect.

Next there are speeches to make. *Compose yourself*, I think. *Tell them what it means. Thank them for everything – don't stuff that up.* After that there are questions to answer and photos to smile for, and these commitments stretch out before me into the night. It's after midnight when a car takes me into the city, to the party where all my people are gathered. So many people who have meant so much to me – it would be impossible to name them all.

I see my fitness team – Tubs and Narelle, Matty and Mel – the people who built me up and kept me going and made me strong. I see my teammate and my captain – Casey and Mol – who held me close and demanded more of me. I see my manager, Nikki, and Benny – the couple who kept me on track. I see my mindset coach and my first coach – Crowey and Jim – the boys who taught me the right life lessons at the right time. I see my tennis gurus – Stolts and Tyzz – who took me to tennis school and helped me graduate with honours. I see my fiancé and my family – Garry and Ali and Sara and Mum and Dad – the ones who picked me up when I fell to pieces, and sacrificed everything so that I might chase a lofty dream. It's the first time all five have been together to see me play, and the first time in a long time that all six of us have been together.

These are the people who brought me to this place, who have been a part of the journey and have brought so much energy. They party hard and go all night long. I can only muster a little energy and I am the first to leave the party. It's time for the people I love the most to enjoy this together. It's time for me to take it all in and get some sleep.

Why, Not When

I need to tell the world about my decision to leave tennis, but first I need to tell *my* world. I sit down with Tyzz and Nikki at home in Brisbane in March 2022.

We sit at the dining table at home, having sushi for lunch and coffee afterwards. It's now that I cry about my choice for the first time, although not because I'm sad about leaving tennis but rather because this is the end of something. The second phase of my career was something we started together, seven long years ago. I was dipping my toe back in the game, while Nikki was going out on her own and Tyzz was taking a chance on me, and now we're going out, on top, together. That's a giant thing to share.

I want to make sure they understand why I am doing this.

'I've achieved my dreams,' I say. 'Not many people in their life get to live out all their dreams.'

I wait for a response, and they just wrap their arms around me.

Don't cry 'cos it's over, I think. *Smile because it happened.*

Garry knows already, and he loves me for my decision. Crowey knows, and he supports me. My family know, and they know it's the right thing, too. The kids are pumped, of course, although Lucy especially needs to confirm it with me.

'But ... when are you going back to play tennis?' she asks.

'I'm not, darling.'

'But … when are you going away again?'

'I'm not.'

'Oh … cool,' she says. 'So we can have some tennis lessons?'

I watch the cogs turn in her brain as she begins to grasp that Aunty Ash is gonna be around a lot more.

Later, I sit down with Casey to film an interview about my choice. This chat is Nikki's idea. She knew that I wouldn't want to do a press conference straight away – that I would want to describe my reasons in my own words.

Before we start the interview, Casey flicks through her notes.

'This is getting real,' she says, and her eyes go glassy. 'You know we don't have to do this.'

'Don't you do it to me, mate,' I say, looking at her as she wells up. 'If you cry, I'll cry.'

We can't look at one another now. Our relationship has always been relaxed – we don't do hard and heartbreaking.

The filming begins and we get very serious very quickly, and we can't stop. It's a strange balance of sad but animated, painful tears and happy tears, talking to one another and talking over one another. The video the public will see is cut down to six minutes and six seconds, but actually we've talked on camera for two and a half hours.

The day before we release the video, there are phone calls I need to make to people I love who I want to hear this message from me first. Narelle. Mol. Mel. Tubs. Storm. Carolyn Broderick, a TA doctor. Chris Mahony, from the national academy in Brisbane. Adam Schuhmacher, my physio at home. Donna Kelso, from the WTA. Micky Lawler, president of the WTA.

The first one is Stolts, and it's hard. He's taken aback.

'Oh, mate,' he says. 'I feel like we've had this conversation before.'

Jim is one of the last, and he says he knew already,

in his gut. 'I had a feeling,' he says. 'I had a feeling after Wimby, and after AO I knew.'

These are the toughest phone calls I've ever had to make, and yet really the hard part is dialling the numbers. When we get to talking, they're easy, because no one is upset or angry. I wouldn't have grown into the person I am without them.

I tell my sponsors and formally inform the tour, and let particular journalists know what is happening. Garry and I go grocery shopping before the video drops, to make sure we have enough food, knowing we won't be leaving the house for the day. We know to close all the blinds, too, because people will come. Other than that, there's nothing to do but wait.

This feels effortless. Light. Natural. My life is going to be exactly the way it has been during the two blissful months since the Australian Open. The only difference is that everyone else will get to know what I'm thinking, and why I'm thinking it, and I want them to have that understanding.

I listen to a lot of athletes talk about their decision to stop competing, because it's a decision most of them will have to make. 'When you know, you know,' they say. And I know.

There's a line I like about this: 'Retire when they ask *Why?*, not *When?*'

Give it away when everyone will ask *Why did you?* rather than *Why don't you?*

That's what I'm doing.

Nikki finally hits send from my social media accounts, and I watch as the messages flow in. The messages came like a raging river after the French Open. Like the sea after Wimbledon. Like the ocean after the Australian Open. But this is more like rain – a seemingly infinite summer storm, showering over this one place in time.

I set my phone to DO NOT DISTURB, because it's too hard to figure out whether I should respond to this one or that one. Do I get back to Scott Morrison and Anthony Albanese right away? In what order do I reply to Cathy Freeman and Hugh Jackman, Mark Webber and Adam Scott? My best mates from the tour – Jules and Kiki and Coco and Simo and Caro and Petra – will understand if I wait a little while before getting back to them. As will every girl I played cricket with at the Brisbane Heat and the Queensland Fire, and the men and women and boys and girls I played with in social competitions as a teenager and child.

The only phone call I take is from Evonne.

'You okay?' she asks.

'Yeah, I'm great.'

'That's all that matters.'

I shut off the news, too. I try to keep myself occupied and pretend to be ignorant of the biggest announcement of my life so far. In the next few days I'll sit down to reply to every single message I've received, because it's important to me to acknowledge their time and their gestures.

What makes me breathe easiest is a simple grab Ali sends me from Twitter. It's not written by her but by someone I don't know. 'The day I retire,' it reads, 'I hope people talk about me the way they're talking about Ash Barty right now.'

That's cool. I've always wanted to make people proud for the right reasons, and I begin to slowly see that the world has received me in exactly that way. The things people are saying about me now have nothing to do with the trophies, the rankings, the matches or even the shots. They're about the behaviour for which I wanted to be known – the friends and the lessons and the memories they have of me.

Ash Barty the tennis player made this announcement, but the responses to it were for Ash Barty the person. It's proof yet again that the two can coexist, overlap and ultimately join. The story and the self are finally together, side by side.

Postscript

Reaching this point in my life – retiring at 25, as the number 1 female tennis player in the world, coming off victory in the 2022 Australian Open – feels like real good fortune. *Seriously, pinch me.* But it's also worth noting that none of this happens – not one bit of it – without that match against Daria Kasatkina at Wimbledon in 2018. That collapse was ground zero, or rock bottom, or whatever you want to call it.

I'll call it base camp – a low vantage point from which I could study the terrain, before attempting to scale the summit. I understand so many things now that I didn't back then.

I understand that it requires not only work, but the constant reinforcement of checking your decisions and interrogating your motivations. More importantly, I understand that tennis doesn't define me, and that I have different dreams outside of the lines of the court.

What I'm going to do with my time isn't settled yet, and in truth I hope it will always remain flexible. I know I want to talk to children through books, and to corporate leaders through speaking engagements. I don't think I want to coach, but I definitely want to mentor. Enough people have helped me find my path – the very least I can do is work on the guidance and growth of others through the lessons I've learned from so many great minds.

I've set up a charitable trust: The Ash Barty Foundation. I want to help people bring out the best in themselves, and be comfortable within themselves, through the pillars of youth, education and sport. I want to help kids across Australia, by giving them opportunities to live out their dreams.

Maybe there's a teenage girl in remote Western Australia who thinks she's fast enough to win the Stawell Gift, but needs some new running spikes and a return flight east to test her mettle. Maybe there's a young golfer in Sydney who wants to play in America, but it'll cost $15,000 for him to chase that dream. I'm hoping they can apply for funding and sponsorship, and we can look at those applications – reading stories both heartbreaking and inspiring – and find a few new ways to expand horizons through resources and opportunities. I can't wait.

But I'm also retired, and I want to take my new-found freedom out for a spin, to see what it can do. When I gave up tennis the first time, Evonne called me and told me it was a good decision, and to 'Go and wet a line'. But I never did. I haven't been fishing in years, but I'd like to. I'd like to go pump the flats somewhere for yabbies, fish off the beach and then see if I can land a big reef fish out off the Great Barrier Reef.

I don't go out a lot, but I'd like to with Jim. One of the things he said when I told him it was over was that we've finally got one more reason to go to the Brekky Creek Hotel and celebrate with a steak. Jim's excited about that, and I am too.

In the months after my Australian Open win and my retirement, many people wondered aloud if I'd go back to the game someday, or maybe have another go at cricket. 'Maybe you should try AFLW,' they suggested. 'You're big into golf – are you going to go pro and join the LPGA Tour?' I'm not, but I do travel a little in those first few months, to play a golf tournament at Liberty National Golf Course in New Jersey, and then at a pro-am event on the Old Course at St Andrews in Scotland before the British Open. For a weekend hacker, I'm spoiled rotten.

I have no desire to play golf professionally – I'm just playing the sport that's always been closest to my family's heart. Mum and Dad met through golf, just as Garry and I did. It doesn't stir my competitive juices – to me it's about having a stroll and having a hit and maybe a laugh, too. It's been funny trying to get people to understand that.

The simple things in life still draw me in. I still love to train and I suspect I always will. I get in the gym and on my bike and I run. Now I feel a freedom to move that's both metaphorical and literal. I need the sweat, too, and that sense of clearing my head through physical exhaustion while listening to random playlists – the trashier the better. After 20 years of training, I get antsy if I do nothing for too long. Maybe I'm addicted to the endorphins.

I'll continue to grapple with the idea that tennis is not who I am but what I did for a while, and that now it's time to do something else for a while. I get questions about that from others, too – 'How's the transition been?' – and the way they ask is always tinged with suspicion, as if I must have some kernel of regret. But this ending is not something that happened to me – it's something I made happen. It's not a breakup, or a breaking point. It's not a tragedy. The circle is complete. My life is as it was and should be. I just don't hit tennis balls for a few hours every day anymore. *I'm good, mate. I'm good.*

I love to relax at home most of all, lingering in my lounge, the dogs chilling on the floor and barking at the wind. I love seeing Garry at the BBQ on the back deck, and me on salad duty in the kitchen. We don't do big dinners or big parties – a quiet night in is a good time. I love cleaning my house, making it spotless and doing it myself. I vacuum the floors last because that's the most satisfying part of the job for me. I always light a scented candle afterwards.

The kids come over all the time. Lucy calls and asks the inevitable question – 'Can I have a sleepover?' – and I respond the same way every time – 'Of course you can, babe – come on over!' What I love most about those moments is that they're no longer special. They are special, of course, but now they're also normal. They aren't rare.

* * *

For Lucy's sixth birthday, she wants a tennis party, so we take her and three best friends back to the West Brisbane Tennis Centre. Mum and Dad and Ali and Sara come down as well. It's 30 minutes of games and then pizza and cake.

'Have a look at Luce,' I say to Jim. 'She's had three lessons.'

He nods, and takes her over to the side of Court 4, just like he did with me 20 years ago. He throws her a ball and – *bang* – she middles it perfectly. Jim's jaw just about hits the ground, and his eyes go as big as I've ever seen. He tries a few combos – *forehand, backhand, switch-switch-switch* – to see what she can do, and we all laugh and shake our heads at the thought.

Jim is selling the centre soon, though, so I come back one weekend before it changes hands. I bring my trophies and we sit them all on a glass outdoor table, and we have a BBQ on the grassy hill in the shade of the tall palms and big jacarandas and giant poincianas. Jim and I have a final hit together on Court 4. We play a few points, and he shows me a thing or two. I'll never stop wanting to learn. I'll never stop loving the game.

Our last shot each is a slice backhand, then Jim walks to the net and rolls it up for the final time. And that's when I lose it, stifling a sob session at the thought of everything that has come to pass since I first set foot here as a baby girl. He gives me the net, because he can see that I need it as a keepsake.

I don't think I'll ever be able to drive back down this road now, because I can't bear the thought that this place, my home, won't be here anymore. I don't want to see it as anything other than how it exists in my mind. When I walked onto those courts as a kid, I felt so small, as if I was lost in this big, scary place, and then the world got bigger and scarier – brighter and wilder and more confusing and more wonderful – while those courts only felt more and more comforting and safe.

I walk each one of them now, and the memories pop back into my mind. I'm practising the slice and mastering the hopper. I'm spitting the dummy and getting angry. I'm gloating and crying. I'm laughing and roaring.

I'm breathing deeply and sweating in the Brisbane sun, chasing yet another ball deep into the corner, turning on the scratchy surface in the shadows and unleashing a final shot. I watch the ball clear the net and land before it bounces, and bounces, and rolls, and stops.

Thank You

My tennis journey and the story I have shared with you in this book would not have been possible without the love and support, belief and talent of so many people –

Mum & Dad • Sara, Lucy & Oscar • Ali, Nick, Olivia & Gabriella • Garry • Steve & Jenny-Lee Kissick • Nikki & Ben Mathias • Jim Joyce • Rob & Sarah Joyce • Craig & Sue Tyzzer • Jason & Andrea Stoltenberg • Narelle Sibte & Shannon Nettle • Casey Dellacqua & Amanda Judd • Mark Taylor • Matthew Hayes • Ben & Sally Crowe • Alicia Molik • Adam Schuhmacher • Melanie Omizzolo • Dr Carolyn Broderick • Dr Robyn

Shirlaw • Evonne Goolagong Cawley & Roger Cawley • Cathy Freeman • Matt Hornsby • Trent & Brooke Cotchin • Andrew Roberts • Darren McMurtrie • Pat Rafter • Donna Kelso • Micky Lawler • Neil Robinson • Victoria Bush • Chris Mahoney • Mark Woolley • John Hamilton • Damien McKern • Luisa Braun • Bill & Elizabeth Peers • John & Sally Peers • Andy Richards • Ian & Karin Codd • Martin Mulligan Sr, Thomas Bischof & my wonderful sponsors • Konrad Marshall, Leo Schlink & the team at HarperCollins

To my playing peers, thank you for pushing me to become the best I could be. Especially to my closest friends: Julia Görges • Kiki Bertens • Petra Kvitova • Storm Sanders • Simona Halep • Coco Vandeweghe • Victoria Azarenka • Caroline Garcia • Caroline Wozniaki • Demi Schuurs • Iga Świątek

And to my fans, thank you for being part of this story too.

Photo Credits

Page 1
All photos Barty family collection

Page 2
Junior Wimbledon
1. © Getty Images/Sean Dempsey
2. © Newspix/Glenn Barnes

Cricket
© Getty Images/
Michael Dodge – CA

Page 3
Representing Australia
1. © Getty Images/Clive Brunskill
2. © Getty Images/Matt King

Teamwork
© Tennis Australia/Fiona Hamilton
© Tennis Australia/Fiona Hamilton

Page 4
WTA tour
1. © Getty Images/Stanley Chou
2. © Getty Images/Clive Brunskill

Page 5
Doubles
© Getty Images/Al Bello

Page 5 (cont.)
French Open
1. © Getty Images/Frey/TPN
2. © Getty Images/Clive Brunskill

Page 6
Wimbledon
1. © Getty Images/Glyn Kirk
2. © Getty Images
3. © Ash Barty personal collection
4. © Getty Images/Peter Nicholls

Page 7
Australian Open
1. © Getty Images/Quinn Rooney
2. © Tennis Australia/Scott Barbour

First Nations community
© Tennis Australia/Scott Barbour

Page 8
Family
2. Nic Morley
All other photos, Barty family collection

The future
© HarperCollins

Australian tennis superstar ASH BARTY teams up with Jasmin McGaughey and Jade Goodwin to bring young readers this fun and exciting new illustrated series about school, sport, friendship and family.

THE WORLD OF Little ASH

COLLECT THE SERIES!

BOOK 1
Ash tries EVERYTHING, but which SPORT will she choose?

BOOK 2
A FRIEND in need? Ash to the RESCUE!

BOOK 3
Ash is in TROUBLE. Will she make her match in TIME?

BOOK 4
Ash is WORRIED she won't WIN ever again!

BOOK 5
Dress-up is FUN but will Ash find her MISSING racquet?

BOOK 6
Ash is having no LUCK. Will she still PLAY hockey?

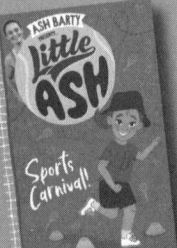

BOOK 7
No tennis? Will Ash still TRY her BEST at the carnival?

BOOK 8
What MISCHIEF can Ash and her new PUPPY get into?

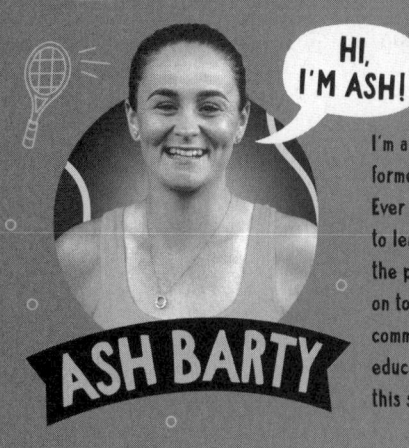

HI, I'M ASH!

ASH BARTY

I'm a three-time Grand Slam singles champion and former WTA World No. 1! I have always loved reading. Ever since I was a little girl, reading has been a way to learn, and has brought me great enjoyment. Over the past few years, reading was a huge part of my life on tour with tennis. I'm a proud Indigenous woman, committed to supporting kids through sport and education around Australia. I'm thrilled to bring you this series of books about a sporty kid, just like me!

HI, I'M JASMIN!

JASMIN McGAUGHEY

I'm a Torres Strait Islander and African American writer and editor. I've always loved storytelling, and I'm proud to be able to work and learn in this field. It has been really exciting to write the Little Ash series. I really hope you enjoy Little Ash's adventures!

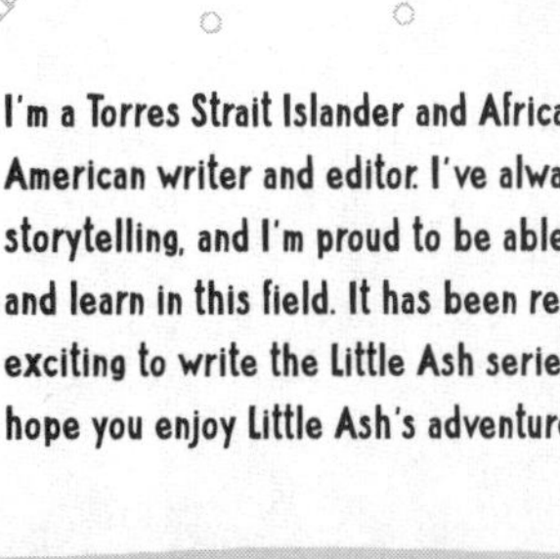

HI, I'M JADE!

JADE GOODWIN

I'm an illustrator, letterer and arts worker. I loved spending time in my grandparents' screen-printing studio when I was growing up. That's why I'm passionate about creating unique and colourful artwork. I use traditional and digital mediums to make my art and I enjoy exploring new ways to connect to my Gamilaraay heritage. I hope you like my drawings in this book!